D1180398

Howard Hodgkin, *Books*, oil on wood, 1991-1995 © The Estate of Howard Hodgkin.

Dear Howard

David Batterham, 2018. Photograph by Tom Miller.

Dear Howard

TALES TOLD IN LETTERS

DAVID BATTERHAM

WITH A FOREWORD BY BARRY HUMPHRIES

REDSTONE PRESS

Published by Redstone Press
7a St Lawrence Terrace,
London W10 5SU
www.theredstoneshop.com

Designed by Julian Rothenstein
with Otis Marchbank
Printed and bound by CPI Books

First edition published as *Among Booksellers*
by Stone Trough Books, 2011

A catalogue record for this book is
available from the British Library

ISBN 978 0995518100

To my sons

Inigo, Aaron, Luke and Thomas

CONTENTS

FOREWORD BY BARRY HUMPHRIES

'I think you are ready for this now Mr Humphries'

I WAS A SCHOOLBOY of 16 when Mrs Ellis Bird, my preferred vendor of secondhand books, placed on the counter a copy of *South Wind* by Norman Douglas. It cost two shillings and sixpence. Mrs Bird's shop was at the top of Burke Street, not far from Parliament House and only a short walk from the Catholic Cathedral. Not seldom, when I visited her book-encumbered shop, I would find her sharing a sherry with a cherubic priest from St Patrick's. She always had a book for me, and to be addressed as 'Mr Humphries' was a tremendous compliment to a schoolboy and a certain guarantee that whatever the book proffered, I would buy it.

Mrs Bird seemed to know and understand the erratic trajectory of my taste. Looking at my shelves today over sixty years later I still see acquisitions inspired so long ago by that sapient old lady in Melbourne. My shelves of Ann Radcliffe and Charles Maturin and William Beckford would not exist if Mrs Bird had not, with her customary reticence proclaimed that I was 'ready' for a pièce de la résistance: *The Monk* by M. G Lewis. I can see it now on her dusty counter:

> Three Volumes. Twelve mo. V, [ii], 232; [ii], 287, [1]; [ii], 315, [i] pp., with publisher's advertisement as final page of volume iii, paper watermarked 1796. Full contemporary tree calf, spines gilt in compartments with plain rules and two morocco labels; some minor

worming touching the first and last few leaves and end-papers of vol. 1, rear joint of vol. 1 nearly invisibly strengthened, vols. 2 & 3 with repairs to upper corner of lower covers, a few leaves lightly soiled in vol. 2.

'Why must you buy all these old books?' complained my mother, 'you don't know where they've *been*!' Of course, that was the reason I loved them, because I had to imagine where they had been, and sometimes there were clues: inscriptions, dedications, bookplates and occasionally tipped-in letters. In those days Melbourne was full of secondhand bookshops because secondhand books were cheaper than new ones; now it's the other way around. When I came to London in the late 1950s and discovered Cecil Court I was in heaven but without the money to buy everything that caught my eye. I didn't know David Batterham then; perhaps he was yet to be born, but he was to become distinguished in booksellers' circles and now we have, handsomely printed, a collection of his absorbing letters to the artist Howard Hodgkin. It is a vivid self-portrait by a knowledgeable man and a testimony to the love of books, which Logan Pearsall Smith called 'that polite and unpunished vice'.

There will come a time, perhaps in my lifetime, when my grandchildren may ask the question 'what is a bookshop?' but I hope not. I used to love the library in my old school where I think I learnt more after school hours than I did in the classroom. It no longer exists. The books are gone and in the library's place is something called a Research and Leadership Centre. But if, in some remote suburb you can find a secondhand bookshop which is not just stuffed with old John Grisham and Judith Krantz paperbacks, but the *real thing*, stand quietly and listen. One day you might just hear a faint dusty voice calling 'I am here! Look up! I am wedged between Vol. 2 of *The Ordeal* by William Clissold and a set of limited signed George Moores (what secondhand bookshop doesn't have a set of those!). Heed this *cri de coeur* and rescue it if you can. It is the plaintive voice of the book you have been searching for all your life. It is a voice that can only be heard in a bookshop.

Never online.

INTRODUCTION

BOOKSELLERS ARE OFTEN rather odd. This is not surprising since we have all managed to escape or avoid more regular forms of work.

It is also a trade for which there are no rules. It can be conducted from a shop in Bond Street, from a barrow or from a car boot. Some booksellers get most of their books from sales, some by clearing houses; others, like myself, simply by buying books from other booksellers' shops.

Before I sold books I sold wallpaper and before that I worked for a firm that imported spray-guns. I became a bookseller by chance. I met Richard Booth at a party and he offered me a job. He later became celebrated as the inventor of the concept of the 'book town' and more specifically for the publicity stunt of declaring himself 'The King of Hay'. Hay-on-Wye, on the Welsh border, became the first book town as Richard's flair for publicity attracted more and more booksellers until there was little room for other businesses.

At the time I joined Richard in 1965 he spent much of the time travelling the country in his maroon Rolls, visiting the people who had responded to the circulars offering to buy books, with which we blanketed the country.

I stayed at the Castle in Hay where I was in charge of selling. Richard gave me a few tips about how this should be done and left me to it.

The few booksellers who made the long journey to Hay must

have done very well as I was completely inexperienced. Most of my time was spent making catalogues which we sent to libraries and other booksellers. I typed these onto sheets of waxed paper and the lists were produced on a duplicating machine.

After a few months Richard gave me the sack for selling the books too cheaply, but by then I could see how I could make a living without returning to paid employment.

I continued to make duplicated lists. At first I bought books mainly by placing an advertisement in the small ads section of *The Times* (in those days on the front page). I was also offered some interesting private collections through friends and family connections. But from 1972 I found my books by making frequent visits to Paris (and other parts of France) and Brussels, later adding Spain and Portugal to my catchment area and also making several trips to America, Denmark, Holland and Finland.

As I didn't have a shop, I worked on the principle that, if I only bought things that I liked, I could eventually gather enough customers with similar tastes to make a catalogue effective. If asked, I say that I specialise in 'books one can enjoy without having to read': trade catalogues, fashion magazines and other illustrated journals, typography, political caricatures, architectural pattern books, the applied arts; no poetry, history or literature.

I occasionally travelled with a girlfriend, and later sometimes with my wife Val, but mostly I was on my own, which is why I got into the habit of writing these letters to Howard. It was not a 'correspondence' since I neither expected nor received any replies.

But I did have him in mind as I wrote, an absent listener or companion, which influenced the kinds of thing I wrote about and particularly the way in which I wrote, the tone and point of view.

I wrote mostly in the evenings as I ate my supper, or in cafés and bars, using up the lonely hours when shops were shut, which is why I should not have been so surprised to find so many references to drink when I came to make this selection. And I now recall that once when I apologised for the wine stains on the page Howard suggested, 'Don't worry; that page can be the frontispiece when you publish them in a book.' So perhaps a wider readership was in the back of my mind, or Howard's – it is thanks to his having kept the letters that I can make this little book.

I first met Howard through Kasmin, the influential and innovative art dealer of the 1960s. His gallery in New Bond Street showed Howard's work and that of David Hockney, Anthony Caro, and others. He and Howard also travelled to India together and arranged a number of exhibitions of Indian miniatures. Paul Kasmin, Sam Hodgkin and my son Aaron were born on consecutive days in 1960 and our families were friends.

In 1967 the Hodgkins and the Kasmins rented the château de Carennac in the Dordogne for a month and invited various friends to join them. There was plenty of room as the place had been a hotel and was fully equipped with cupboards full of linen, a huge kitchen, dining room, breakfast room, etc. It was here that I first got to know Howard well. The atmosphere was fairly fraught with so many people trying to get on with each other. I remember a meeting with Howard by the tap in the basement where we were trying to get a shave and his commenting, 'This place is like a private looney bin'. His remark and point of view perhaps find an echo in these letters written in later years.

DAVID BATTERHAM,
ALEXANDER STREET, W2

FRIENDS AND FAMILY IN THE TEXT

Craigie Aitchison (1928–2009), painter.

Inigo Batterham, son of DB, painter.

Thomas Batterham, son of DB.

Tim Behrens (1937–2016), artist.

Serge Brodsky, film maker.

Richard Burton (1933–2017), architect, early work included in Kasmin Gallery in New Bond Street, schoolfriend of DB.

Bruce Chatwin (1940–89), writer, friend of HH.

Caroline Conran, writer and journalist married to Terence Conran at time of letters.

Terence Conran, furniture designer, founder of Habitat, restaurateur.

Polly Devlin, writer and journalist, sister of Val Devlin.

Val Devlin, wife of DB.

Captain Foulenough, character in J. B. Morton's 'Beachcomber' column in the Daily Express, known for stealing cats.

Andy Garnett (1930–2014), businessman, founder of electronics firm Radiodetection, husband of Polly Devlin.

Henry Geldzahler (1936–94), art historian and New York museum curator.

Marie Heaney, wife of Seamus; sister of Val and Polly Devlin.

Sam Hodgkin, son of HH.

Kasmin, former gallery owner, traveller and collector.

Jane Kasmin, mother of Paul Kasmin.

Paul Kasmin, gallery owner in New York.

Jack Lane (1899–1979), father of Julia Hodgkin, wife of HH at the time of these letters.

Paul Levy, food writer, friend of HH.

Alistair (later Lord) McAlpine, (1942 – 2014), art collector, former owner of Erasmus bookshop in Cork Street, London.

Stephanie Maison (1918–2008), director of art dealers Hazlitt, Gooden and Fox.

François de Menil, scion of Houston art-collecting family, later an architect in New York.

Richard Morphet, former Keeper of the Modern Collection at the Tate Gallery, writer, friend of HH.

Jasper Morrison, furniture and product designer.

Danny Moynihan, painter, novelist, one-time partner in Space Gallery, London, with Paul Kasmin and Jasper Morrison.

Jules Olitsky (1922–2007), Russian/American artist whose work was shown by both Kasmin and Paul Kasmin.

Antony Peattie, partner of HH.

Vera Russell (*née* Poliakoff, 1911–92), Russian actress and later writer on art; married art critic John Russell (her third husband); mother of Richard Burton, above.

Tom Schiller, comedian, director, film maker, best known for series of short films made for the American TV show 'Saturday Night Live'.

Dr Efim Shapiro worked for the BBC Russian Service.
Heathcote Williams (1941–2017), playwright and poet.
Michael Williams, artist and teacher at the time of these letters.
Brian Young, artist and teacher.

PLACES AND BOOKS IN THE TEXT

Bertorelli's. Famous Italian restaurant in Charlotte Street, 'Fitzrovia', London, now closed.

Marshfield. Small Wiltshire town close to HH's home in Castle Combe.

Picture Post, 1938–57. Important weekly photo-journal founded by Stefan Laurent and edited by Tom Hopkinson. Photographers including Bert Hardy, Felix Mann, Kurt Hutton, and Bill Brandt provided an unrivalled picture of Britain during the Second World War and post-war period.

L'Assiette au Beurre, 1900–12. Delightful magazine of social and political satire, each issue on a separate theme and illustrated by a single artist. It consisted almost entirely of illustrations. This was a particularly rich time for illustrators including some, such as Juan Gris, Franz Kupka and Félix Valloton, more widely known as artists.

Le Témoin, nos. 1–69, 1933–35. Editor: Paul Iribe. Satirical review started as a reaction to the evils of Communism, Nazism, American influence and the perceived feebleness of the French government. Hyper-nationalistic, right-wing, anti-democratic stuff, beautifully presented. Paul Iribe wrote most of it himself and provided most of the drawings. As a sustained outpouring of political and polemical satire,

Le Témoin is one of the great twentieth-century journals in this genre.

E. A. Séguy's *Papillons* (1928). The *pochoir* method of illustration was used mainly in France in the early twentieth century. Colours were applied by hand through stencils, producing a particularly thick, richly coloured surface. There were many portfolios, often of patterns for use by decorators. *Pochoir* was also used for book illustration.

SEM. The *nom de plume* of George Goursat (1863–1934), artist of albums such as '*Le Vrai et le Faux Chic*' and '*Black Bottoms*' caricaturing society life.

LETTERS

SAN ANTONIO, Texas, August 1970

Dear Howard,
My sister recommended this hotel but she was here in February.
I didn't notice until I got up to my room that the neon sign over
the hotel door did not say 'All Rooms Air Conditioned' but 'All
Rooms Air Cooled', which means there is a huge fan churning up
the air in an attempt to disguise the temperature, which is about
90. It also blows the ash in the ashtray over the table.

Dallas International Airport, Sunday morning
Palm Court music wafting through artificial marble halls. Everyone
here is washed, shaved and deodorised. We are almost a different
race from Homo Greyhound. Certainly the environment encourages
me to think I must have gone through some evolutionary process. I
need it after last night. That hotel had a mysterious sort of Graham
Greene charm. Very high ceilings, peeling wallpaper, dim fly-blown
lights, archaic wooden fittings. But so hot. Like a cloud of dust.
Upstairs light glowed through the louvred doors of the rooms and
there was a humming of fans and the sound of dripping taps. I
worked out a system to keep cool by soaking a towel in cold water,
wrapping it round me like a poultice and then letting the fan blow
on me. But obviously I couldn't keep it up while I was asleep. So
I had to go out again. In Greene's book I would have gone to a
run-down brothel where the madam, a former NAAFI manager
from Alexandria and a dear old friend, would have given me iced

tea and so forth. But I just went through the nearest padded door into a windowless barn and sat at a long bar.

A huge bald slob next to me consulted me about whether he should get a wig. 'My sister says I should. Most of my friends have them. Just for special occasions like church on Sunday.' So we got very pally; and I gradually got to accept the constant grasping of my shoulder, squeezing of my arm, slapping of my leg and the beery breath too near my ear. We went on to another bar where there was a blind pianist. 'Always moves me, him being blind and all!' Here I was taken on by a Baptist lay preacher, just retired from the army, who offered to show me a place not two blocks from here where Mexican children were starving to death, and related how he had sat on his porch with a shotgun to protect his family from raids by the Ku Klux Klan.

By 2 am I had cut down the sleeplessness that lay ahead to an acceptable four hours ...

Gurney's Hotel, Santa Barbara, 1970
The art shop here offers 'boutiquing kits' and a handbook recommending that 'foam fruit tastefully dangled will make an iridescent conversation piece.'
Love, David

HAMMAMET, Tunisia, 1973

Dear Howard,

This is the strangest 'buying trip', I imagine, that I will ever have the chance to make.

It is quite hard work being here although there is really nothing to do. I had looked at the books before breakfast on my first day; but there are certain rituals that I have to go through, of studying, appreciating, appraising, etc. On the other hand I cannot really relax because there is the difficult problem of getting the books back to England. I think today I am beginning to get it organised. Mahmoud the major domo/cook has summoned the postman here this morning on his moped and we've had a long discussion about parcels. The postman is one of 'Mah Boys' and gave my host a reverential kiss on his flaking cheek when he shuffled into our discussion in his pyjamas. If the worst comes to the worst I will just have to leave my clothes behind and should be able to get the 55 volumes of *Curtis's Botanical Magazine* into my suitcase.

I wake at about 6 am after a restless sleep interrupted by croaking frogs and roaring and bellowing peacocks. This morning it was a Siamese cat screaming like a baby outside my door.

I opened the door to let it in but it didn't want to come in; it jerked its head for me to follow it, which I did nervously thinking it wanted me to deliver some kittens, but it just stalked across the courtyard and sat down by a hole. I nodded in a friendly way and it stopped screaming.

At about 7 I am brought a cup of coffee and the shutters are opened and I have to get up.

I walk a little in the garden and mooch about in the library, a small octagonal room with sandalwood shelves and a tall pointed ceiling. This morning I went with Mahmoud into the town to get some cardboard boxes and string. Then to the beach for a swim. Most of the coast is densely built up with hotels so this last relic of the open dunes is particularly popular with beach-boys or whatever they are called. A jolly ten-year-old offered to fuck me in about six languages, and then his brother who was about three inches taller took over and explained that his brother was a rude bad boy, and 'where is your wife?' and besides he is too small, while he himself is much bigger and better. Finally they joined forces and offered me two big men for a pound.

Returning from my swim at noon I have the first of my daily meetings with my weird old host. You may be surprised to hear it but I believe one of my recommendations for this assignment was that I am a good listener. I will soon be very good. I join the old Ageing Beauty, as I call him, on the patio outside the drawing room. He is sitting in the sun, his blue swollen feet stretched out in front of him, one hand hidden by his paunch somewhere down between his legs and his other hand caressing his face, soothing away the wrinkles with coconut oil.

We have our drinks and he drones on about his life and Life. I don't say much but I think he likes me because he told me that the servants, 'Mah Children', had decided I was a relation on his mother's side. He is the most completely self-centred and self-absorbed person I have ever met. I am gradually piecing together some kind of picture of his life, probably wildly wrong.

He is American, about 75, from Georgia, and called Jean (pronounced Gene) Henson. He talks quite a lot about 'niggras' and very slowly with what must be the remnant of a Southern drawl. 'I was a beautiful boy, David; in Paris in 1921 and wherever I went, doors opened. I've been lucky David. And not just lucky. I'm intelligent, an intuitive animal ... ' It all drones on. 'When I first saw Cocteau I decided to seduce him.' 'I knew them all; they all knew me' is his chief refrain.

The names drift about like dried leaves. Most have an unfamiliar ring. Old women who once fancied him, I suppose, and boys, boys, boys. 'He was Mah Friend, David.'

'I have always loved two things, David, women and boys'. From Paris he moved on to Capri and then to Taormina and eventually to Hammamet. And on the way he met 'Mah Violet' and married her. Perhaps she was rich, or perhaps he was. Perhaps I'll hear later about that.

I am being unkind as usual, hoping for a smile, even a laugh; because however they did it and however they managed it, whoever they were or knew, this house is a very remarkable place. Perhaps rather fey and pretentious but very spacious and yet intimate.

It is now time to join Jean for drinks and our evening session and dinner at 7. The cook, a powerful man, very like Nasser to look at, is very good. After dinner we sit very close on a blue sofa in the huge vaulted sitting-room and Jean drones on about how he found this fountain and that fountain ... and how the last young man who looked at the books STOLE some Lovat Fraser drawings. 'That's a Tang horse, David.' A long story that one, and aren't Tang horses worth thousands of pounds?

Love, David

PARIS, May 1974

Dear Howard,

My last letter, from Cornwall, I never sent. Nothing was happening. No one to gossip about. So it was about Art. About you really. I censored it. It could have contained a bit about the Artist's Worry, that however well things are going today, what about tomorrow? Recently I've noticed that this is not a worry confined to artists. It attacks booksellers as well.

And I've noticed, reluctantly, that my overdraft has increased during the last eighteen months from £3,000 to £18,000. This £15,000 doesn't seem to be on my shelves. I am only mildly worried by the thought that I spend £1,000 a month more than I earn.

I've not bought much here but I am pretending this doesn't matter because I am on the track of the bookbinder from whom my collection drawings of decorative 1920s bookbinding designs originated. And in my mind they will wipe out all my debts.

Next day

Pursuing the bookbinder. To the Bibliothèque Nationale to see M. Toulet the Curator of Bookbinding. A wonderful fellow. Charming, amusing, with a grey crew cut like a retired French army colonel; very smart casual clothes. On one of the drawings he found a name, perhaps a signature: Louis Gilbert. He sent a minion to check the computer to see if there were any references to Louis Gilbert in the Library. At last the woman returned with a scrap of paper. 'There are two Louis Gilberts,' said M. Toulet. 'One is the author of a treatise on Catholicism in the 17th century, and the other has written a book on sexually transmitted diseases. Nothing about a bookbinder!' Then he tapped his head and remembered having seen a book bound by Louis Gilbert in the catalogue of a shop in the Blvd Haussmann. This is a shop so pretentious it might have been designed for a film set. Presided over by a man who, though about 30, seemed about 200, as if pickled in vinegar. He'd never heard of Louis Gilbert. But he showed me another bibliography of binders by a M. Devauchelles.

Round the corner was another very smart shop called Blaizot. M. Blaizot is also a bindings man and keeps a shop like a tomb with middle-aged (about my age) ladies sitting at little desks. He consulted books and racked his brains and then arranged that I visit the great M. Devauchelles in his *atelier*. M. Devauchelles was not charming. A bit of a thug. His white coat made me think of surgeons rather than bookbinders. He was scathing and dismissive of my collection of designs but made me suspicious because he said he would like to buy them. 'I have a large collection of maquettes,' he said, indicating an invisible pile about neck high. He even offered to swap them for Volume III of his own book on the subject.

So I have not got much further on. Perhaps a few rungs down on my search for the crock of gold.

But there was a crock of gold a few doors down the Blvd. A marvellous old English woman (from Brighton) and her 89-year-old French husband, who has a face mottled like a snakeskin in an old engraving. She said she had only had the present shop since 1961, 'but my husband has had lots of shops. And wives!' she laughed. Not surprisingly it's not a very active shop but I was allowed into the basement to help get down some theatrical magazines that had been in the shop since they arrived. There was a big table down there and two places laid for a meal. Mme Gonot ('Go Not', she winked) brings their lunch with them and cooks it on a stove. The lease runs out in December but she is not worried. 'My husband finds the driving rather tiring, especially the hairpin bends in the underground car park, so I am looking for another shop nearer to where we live in the 15ème!' Wonderful. I wish you could have been with me.

In fact M. Gonot was not the oldest bookseller I have come across in Paris. This was Arnold Levilliers, a German living on a dreary road at Issy-les-Moulineaux on the outskirts of Paris. He was an expert on Daumier. I called one afternoon without an appointment. His dismal house was set back from the road, his doorbell connected by a wire to a brass knob by the front gate. The bell clanged inside the house. After a while an upper window, a 'casement,' opened and an old man in a night cap over long grey hair looked out. I half expected him to haul up a blunderbuss. But he came down at last in a floor-length dressing gown, like some old actress in her dressing room, with that ghastly hair hanging down. We had a long chat.

He grumbled that his secretary demanded 50 francs an hour, or was it 5Fr? When I left he apologised for having been in bed. 'When you are 94 you will probably want to take a siesta.'
Love, David

VENICE, 16 November 1974

Dear Howard,
However much I travel I remain the world's worst traveller. I never learn. Take this meal for example. If I had taken a few moments' thought I could have bought a simple phrase book giving the true facts about what is on the menu, but I just order blindly with a hopeful air of confidence. I am probably the only person who has ever ordered *zucchini* with this particularly rubbery and bony fish. They may have had the fish for years awaiting my arrival here.

'Here' is a sort of artists 'hotel' with pictures on the walls. Not unlike the Bayswater railings, bent round to form four walls and roofed in. In the summer there is a beautiful courtyard with arched vines. The manager didn't want me to stay here and tried to pretend it was full up—but in fact I am really the only inmate. At least I thought I was until I nipped upstairs just now for some more Anadin and saw another man framed in the door of the gloomy marble floored ping-pong room on the first floor, small and bald. He was wearing Fatty Arbuckle striped pyjamas, with his arms outstretched trying to reach around his circumference with the cords of his dressing-gown. He shot through a door behind the piano.

It is rather trendy in here, though not as trendy as it was at lunchtime; dazzling old bags lunching alone, smoothy-chops business men in fine shades of bright blue entertaining the men from Milano in fine shades of pale grey. (I am wearing my 1964 Jaeger sale jacket with a hole in the elbow and the buttons no longer meeting the button-holes; my Oxfam shop white lambs-wool sweater, back to front because of the wine stains and holes burned by Gauloises debris, and my Cheltenham rotter's trousers) ... which reminds me of my last visit to Cheltenham, a story against myself.

I called to see Peter Barrie in Montpellier Walk. I could hear him upstairs but there was a forbidding string across the staircase so I introduced myself to the man at the desk. I greeted Peter effusively halfway up the stairs. Peter was not effusive, at all, at all! He asked my name again. I repeated it.

'What firm are you from?'

'I'm not a firm. I'm David Batterham.'

'You said that before. What's your firm?'

'I see you have forgotten my name, Peter.'

'Yes, I have.'

'And my face. It is only two months since I was here last.'

'I have seen a lot of faces in two months.'

'Sorry, Peter; it doesn't seem a very convenient moment.'

'No, it's not. Frank, if anyone else asks for me I am with a customer.'

All this with his horrible face, familiar for over ten years, gold teeth, gap teeth, shaven head and white puffy skin, only a foot away but two feet above me since we were on the stairs.

This meeting worried me all the way back to London. Why? What should I have done? If his memory has really gone, should I warn him before he offends all his customers; if it has not gone, should I ask him what grisly story about me is going round the trade?

It sounds as if it is raining outside but it is only an extractor fan. On the other hand if it rains it may flood and my gumboots will be useful; yes, they are weighing down my Revelation suitcase like a sub-machine gun. I've not got a phrase book; I've not read Ruskin or Baedeker; I've forgotten my copy of Augustus Hare's *Venice*. But I have got my two heavy-duty Dunlop, double welted, arty green wellies.

Of course not bothering to find out about Venice before I set off has had its mind-blowing rewards. I once described to you the spine-tingling shock of coming across the contents of

32

Degas' studio in a bedroom at Paul Mellon's house in Virginia; I mentioned the surprise of a friend at finding the carpeted floor of the Blue Mosque in Istanbul, and perhaps no one is ever really prepared for Venice. I'd seen a postcard of the Bridge of Sighs, and done *The Merchant of Venice* at school; Jo's parents lived in Little Venice ...

I arrived here under rather inauspicious circumstances. An eight-hour delay at Luton, my flight diverted to Rimini, a four-hour bus trip, racing along the motorway in a coach with six rather posh package travellers and their professional courier; set down at 2.30 am, led along an alley to a quiet jetty dancing with gondolas, a palace dozing in the moonlight across the canal; a trip along canals, under bridges, to a huge and grand hotel by San Marco (the room cost £18 and by a decimal error I tipped the man who gave me my bill £4. Here my room is £2). And then getting up and walking out into the streets.

'You'll like Venice', people said. 'Venice is lovely', they said. Even 'Venice is the most beautiful place in the world' (of course they couldn't go further than that). It has made me quite ill, frantic with amazement.

The head man here reminds me of Jack. He doesn't look like Jack; it is something about the way he smokes and the flies on his grey flannels, a tilt of his old head, that links him to a line of Ancient Kings.

Now Jack has turned out the lights in the depths of the room. The young waiter, who looks like Sam, in a red and black waistcoat, is talking to his sister on my left, a very beautiful girl. Her fearsome old mother is playing cards with my waiter and some fat old men. In sudden bursts of laughter they become 30, then 20, even back at school – perhaps the one behind the high wall a few streets from here.

The girl has gone to bed, Sam is asleep on his folded arms, Jack is noisily washing some cups.

This afternoon near the quay overlooking the cemetery I saw two very chic girls of about 20 turning into a narrow street just ahead of me. I think they were twins; almost matching grey coats, very expensive long crinkly boots, a sparkle of gold crucifixes, shiny black hair, gleaming teeth, a whiff of scented lambswool, silk and clean underwear. And then there were two schoolgirls with satchels, giggling uncontrollably and intimate; and then, as I hurried along in my old green coat and swinging my plastic bag, I almost knocked down two very old ladies, now shrunk to schoolgirl size, arm in arm, both with sticks, suited, hatted, hair-dyed. I've already tried to squeeze some significance out of this simple scene in a letter to Michael Williams, to catch the scent on Time's old hanky?

Was this very simple meal worth £8? Do I really have to come to Venice to find time to write to you?

Love to you all, David

BARCELONA, 1976 (For Tim Behrens's exhibition)

Dear Howard,

I am in Barcelona. In a café. Somewhere near the port. I can see two towers that seem to carry a cable car across the harbour. I can see some enormous sheds with buttressed walls and tiled roofs; they may be medieval market halls or they may be some 19th century tram depot; it is hard to see from here and my feet are too sore for me to investigate.

I am smoking a French cigar, the cheapest brand there is, called Voltigeur. It is one left over from a supply I fetched from Paris last month as a present for a Very Old Artist, called, believe me, Edmund X. Kapp, a fascinating Jewish gnome, delightfully pleased with himself and absurdly old. He came *down* from Cambridge in 1912 and was Edmund Blunden's commanding officer in the Great War. His chief claim to renown seems to be that he is the only person for whom Picasso actually sat for a portrait. Kapp's account of the occasion was a barefaced masterpiece of anecdote. As he had expected only to have half an hour with Picasso, he decided to make some notes instead of actually doing the drawing. After about three hours Picasso suddenly woke up and asked good-naturedly if he could 'have a look'; but there was nothing to look at, only these 'notes' (pages of noses, eyebrows, Adams apples, I suppose).

Picasso was very understanding and said, 'Well, I've got to go out to tea with Gertrude Stein now, but I'll tell you what. Do the drawing later.' And he signed a huge sheet of paper for the purpose. And then, with a wink, signed a second piece. Kapp was so overawed by these sheets that he kept them from 1936 until 1958 when he finally got round to using one of them for the drawing. He published this as a limited edition together with a little booklet describing his meeting with Picasso. He didn't need the second sheet after all and claims that it is the only large blank sheet of paper signed by Picasso in existence.

Hours later I am thankfully now sitting in a restaurant. It was a relief to get in here as I was beginning to feel somewhat alarmed; little twinges of worry and loneliness, even occasional glimpses, as if through a half-open door, of the giants Despair and Misery laughing at me. I find it very disturbing not being able to speak to anyone or understand anything anyone says.

A few weeks ago I had a dream that there would be books in Barcelona. The vision even showed me where they are. Upstairs, over a sort of W. H. Smith's art shop, is a huge room, 300ft long and filled with books. The shop belongs to four brothers. I only hope I can find it. Dreams are very unreliable: the long gallery may not be in Barcelona at all; in fact it may not exist (well, you needn't be told this). It may not even be a wishing dream. The W. H. Smith's may be my father, the long gallery my mother's womb; the four brothers may be the women in my life or the Four Horsemen of the Apocalypse.

A dream doesn't always lead to action and yet here I am in Barcelona for Tim Behrens's exhibition.

Thursday

Lunch was good. Ten people, five drunk and five sober at a long white table overlooking the beach (a strip of shit-strewn sand in the harbour, surrounded by gasworks and tin shacks). The highpoint came when Craigie Aitchison wavered his way across the sand to sprinkle salt and pepper over … *writing illegible here so the highpoint is lost. Who did he sprinkle?*

Friday 10pm

Things have got very out of hand. Lunch lasted until five when I managed to suggest a trip over the harbour by cable car. Tim's brother produced some huge purple pills to prevent vertigo and since then everyone has been feeling very odd.

I left to go by taxi to a bookshop, a *libreria,* and was taken by the driver to Iberian Airlines!

Then I was woken at 8 pm (thinking it was 8 am) by a distraught girl with palpitations and a man in her bedroom. I took her to supper which she couldn't eat and now she has passed out in my room, and I am here in this 100ft square Oriental Lounge drinking beer at 50p a glass. I have to fetch it myself as the waiters are so scathing.

It is a terrible strain being here with all these people. I think I prefer being so lonely that I have to sit and write letters. My share of the lunch bill was £12 yesterday and today it rose to £18. Tomorrow I am arranging a picnic in the Park Güell.

I don't mind paying for Tim; I hardly mind paying for Serge

Brodsky whose international sponging is of Picasso-like proportions and genius. He recently hitchhiked from Rome to Islington, by train, with three children and a ceramic stove weighing 2 cwt and even found a man to carry it upstairs. I'm less enthusiastic about Paul Getty's girlfriend Victoria who is daily expecting Mr Aitken of Drummond's Bank to cable her some readies ... And as for Patrice! The only person who ordered a special, private pudding, didn't eat it, and became completely deaf when I made loud sarcastic remarks about the bill!

See you soon. Love, David

COPENHAGEN, Thursday 17 April 1977

Dear Howard,

I've just nipped into a bar for my tea; a bottle of lager brewed across the street. It cost 65p, but worth it. It took me some time to recognise a bar. From the street they are all very private and forbidding. Darkened glass with an extractor fan, a flush, padded door with a small grill window. Inside, wooden chandeliers with pimpled plastic shades hang low over tables covered with red cloths. Some mildly drunk old men in green overcoats.

I arrived in Denmark on Easter Sunday and went at once to stay with an old family friend, Ulf Rasmussen. He is an artist, a sculptor. I saw as soon as I got there that he and his environment are my archetypes, subtly hinting at me for the last thirty years. His house is a long low thatched place on the edge of a fjord covered with swans. A romantic highlight of my visit was when Ulf called me into the garden to watch the swans setting off for Siberia where they spend the summer: hundreds of trumpeting birds circled the house a couple of times and then headed north east. We watched them vanish over the horizon like a vast flapping washing line of white shirts. 'They have a fine day,' said Ulf, 'with the wind behind them.'

The garden is full of busts and torsos and there is a muddled yard of sheds full of old iron and wooden trestles and boxes of rusty chisels and trays of little coloured cubes of rock for making mosaics. When I first came here Ulf dug the big garden once a year with a horse-drawn plough and we lived largely on eels which we caught at night with spears by the light of an acetylene lantern fixed on the prow of our dinghy.

Inside, the house is a mid-nineteenth-century still-life, rather bare and uncomfortable. Old furniture, kelims and Afghan rugs on polished boards; a few alabaster heads of babies, some ceramic ducks, jugs of feathers and a lot of muted pictures by Ulf's father-in-law Karl Schou, who was the Utrillo of Scandinavia. Meals are taken at a big table which is set up with Japanese precision for the humblest cup of tea or glass of schnapps.

On Monday it snowed nearly all day and we sat quietly in the room, writing letters at separate tables and listening to a big clock ticking in the passage.

When I left the sun was warmer and Ulf was settling down by a bit of granite weighing ten tons which he'd personally selected from the foot of a glacier in Iceland last summer.

Later

Staying with Richard and Sally Morphet's friends, Klaus and Eva.

I am writing this at 8.30 in the morning having been awake since 6. I had hoped to take the 9 o'clock hovercraft to Sweden but I can't leave without saying goodbye and the family are all still asleep, an hour and a half later than usual. I saw them as I went to the bathroom, a great jumble of duvets and heads and bottoms, gaping mouths and rucked-up nighties, all four of them. But it is nice sitting here writing to you so I will catch the 10 o'clock instead.

I have found a few good books, but a German called Holstein was here last week. In every shop there is a pile waiting to be sent off to him. I feel like a small dog following a big dog from lamp post to lamp post.

I have come across some curious people too. In one shop I found a copy of Muthesius's *Das Englische Haus* which is said to be an excellent book, very expensive. When I asked the price the man said, 'You must put it on the balances.' The books were being sold by weight, £1 per kilo. He told me to come back the next day and look in the basement, where I found a run of *Studio Yearbook of Decorative Art* for 4/- per volume. They can pay for my fare and expenses, and may have to pay for a book about curtains that I carelessly put on the pile for £135.

The pile of Richard's friends is getting up and I must away to Sweden.

Love, David

BUIS-LES-BARONNIES, S. E. France. May 1979

Dear Howard,

I feel as if I have had no sleep at all because of the ceaseless dreams and nightmares that hit me as soon as I have had enough brandies to ensure a good night's rest. One night I was attending the very harrowing death-bed scene of a dreadful German in a grey track suit who lisped out some last words. They seemed to contain the secret of the universe so I made a great effort, staggered out of bed, turned on the neon light in my windowless room and wrote them down on a piece of paper. Next day, when I was finally released from sleep, I found the scrap of paper. Scrawled on it in erratic planchette-type writing was, 'Forget and forgive. Love and be happy.' Sounds rather familiar. Probably rather good advice and oddly coherent, though I'd been expecting something a bit deeper.

Last night I slept a bit better. Took one of the sleeping tablets I had stolen from my father's medicine cupboard (I nearly wrote drinks cupboard—much the same in his house). When I woke up, with my arms round a bolster at the wrong end of the bed, it was too late to have any breakfast.

This morning I spent in the post office trying to arrange to get away from this mountain retreat. The telephone enquiry woman was unhelpful. She spoke very quickly and with a strong accent and when I asked in my gentlemanly way for a slower repetition, she sneered at me, 'Why don't you learn French? It's very easy.' I then went to another telephone hoping to get another operator but it was the same one. She recognised me at once and asked why the hell I bothered to come to France when my French is unintelligible. In the end I had to get the man in the hotel to make my calls for me.

Love, David

NEW YORK, 5 May 1980

Dear Howard,

My own time in NY has been fairly calm, no alcoholic benders, no sex. Hardly even up after bedtime. But not entirely without those bizarre glimpses that only seem to happen abroad. I did find myself dropping into the St Regis Hotel late one evening with Tom Schiller to deliver a birthday present to François de Menil. A kind of Gatsbyish party was roaring along, men in dinner jackets draped with streamers, collars loosened, dreadful Muzaktype disco music. I saw Henry Geldzahler stalking briskly among the tables, looking this way and that as if on a crowded beach trying not to admit that he couldn't find his towel.

I was staying with Tom in his Washington Mews house, though we hardly met, apart from one evening when we watched a film of a 1950s Liberace TV show. Tom remarked to his girlfriend that we were probably the only people in the universe watching the Liberace film, and when the reel ended, it was 'Now no one in the universe is watching Liberace', and it was bedtime.

Love, David

PARIS, June 1981

Dear Howard,

This afternoon I was in the rue de Seine and watching all the art dealers bustling about like fish in an aquarium, and I was wondering who buys it all and what happens to all the unsold pictures. What happened to Jules Olitski? Has Kasmin got a rack of them at Jim Moyes's warehouse? The answer to this rhetorical question was round the next corner. An Olitski exhibition! There they all were: *Nuances* 1968, *Resonance* 1967, *Balance* 1968. And quite a lot of action in the tank. An assistant was holding one work on a chair, the owner in a lilac cardigan gesticulating and making curious kissing movements with his face, and two rich-looking punters in too-nipped-in suits were taking short steps forward then briskly back, their heads rolling first to the left and then to the right.

David

MORECAMBE, 15 January 1982

Dear Howard,

I am in the dining room of the Midland Hotel in Morecambe. The receptionist looked at me doubtfully when I asked if there was a restaurant. 'You'll have to ask the Restaurant Manager if there is a free table.' In fact there is only one other guest in this vast room. I am having the set dinner (£9) and bottle of alcohol-free wine (£5.50 but it is in an ice bucket). My own hotel is along the seafront, the only one with a light over the door in a mile of shut B&Bs on the promenade (£9.95).

No need to go abroad when there are places as strange as this just down the motorway.

The reason I am here is that I was roped in by a friend to answer a 'call out' to some people in Manchester who were alleged to have a set of *Picture Post* and another of *Illustrated* and possibly *Life* and *Men Only* and other eccentric goodies. I had to rent a van and I set out early in pouring rain, feeling rather humiliated by having agreed to join the venture. But by Luton the sun had come out and I felt more cheerful by the time I reached 69 Crumps Lane. This was an almost collapsing seven-bedroom house in a jungle of weeds with dirty, torn net curtains in the windows and a big lorry in the drive with its wheels deep in nettles, or maybe ivy. It belonged to an 82 year-old half-dead antique dealer. His son and daughter were trying to clear the house by the day after tomorrow. They turned down my generous offer of £700 and decided to keep everything if I didn't give them another £200.

Rather to my own surprise I found myself putting on my coat to leave, quite glad not to have to load up all the junk (most of the promised things were not there). At this point old Mr Mendelsohn suddenly snapped into action and ordered them to accept my offer. 'He's got to make a profit', he reminded them.

So although I am not very excited by my van full of old *Blighty* and *Reveille* and *Sunday Times* colour magazines, I feel more cheerful than I might have done. And I have come a bit further north so I can collect a set of the Encyclopedia Britannica from a shop in Lancaster.

The helpings are rather large Up North. But not as large here as they were in Carlisle last month. I ordered some lamb cutlets. A huge oval platter arrived, loaded like a butcher's tray. The service was very genteel, the veg brought separately by the waiter in little divided dishes.

'Some roast potatoes, Sir? A few beans?'

I began to eat.

'Some carrots? Any onions?'

I tried again but he was back.

'Cauliflower cheese? Some ratatouille?'

'A little green salad?'

And finally, 'Would Sir care for a few chipped potatoes?'

Love, David

FRANCE, 1983

Dear Howard,

This evening to see a Dutch bookseller who lives in a small *château* near Saumur. A very smooth fellow I have not seen since I met him in Amsterdam.. He has left the museum where he worked and moved to this very nice house. He offered me a pile of books for £500 but when I demurred he gave me some more wine and made some passes over his calculator. 'I have another proposal. What about £400?' Just OK.

Now that he is living in France he is specialising in salon catalogues from the 1800s. Very good business it seems. And he wants me to find him the first ten years of *The Graphic*, which were owned and loved by Van Gogh.

He wore white cricket trousers, a blue linen jacket and a long scarf which he kept on all the time I was there — quite a long time because I kept thinking they would ask me to dinner. Their assistant Dick was even sent out to buy meat while I was there.

Dick looked very like Brian Young and had a disconcerting habit of plunging his hand into his trousers and ostentatiously adjusting his parts.

Luckily, and surprisingly, there is a *pizzeria* in this tiny village.

The plot thickens. I was just getting into my car this morning when some instinct led me to look at one of the books I had bought from the Dutchman. Sure enough it had a plate missing, a coloured plate. Back to the *château*, glistening in the early sun, the lawns hidden under a layer of mist. A little car was parked outside the open front door. They were all there in the salon, the bookseller now dressed in a green tweed suit with yellow shirt, a red tie and a corduroy cap. They looked an odd, isolated trio, as if they had their bags packed and were waiting for a phone call from Basel or Zurich to tell them that the bank had accepted their false draft and that the money was waiting in the left luggage office. They must have had a shock when they heard my car scrunching on the gravel.

Love, David

LISBON, 1983

Dear Howard,

I had given up drinking for two weeks before I came here. But I have taken it up again as I am so lonely, so you may not be able to read this.

It is enchanting here. I feel giddy trying to put it in a nutshell, on a thumbnail – in this letter.

It is very hilly. Yesterday I thought I was going up a sort of Eiffel Tower and it turned out I was taking the lift to another street, 250 feet above …

There are very few cars. No yellow lines or parking meters – but trams, some very small, like coaches, in varnished wood. On the narrow streets, where there is single-line traffic, there are men with coloured ping-pong bats who sit all day preventing head-on collisions.

And there are terrifying beggars, legless usually, but outside my hotel is an eyeless one, face smooth as a Magritte. And there are flower sellers who bring sacks of wild flowers and grass from the country and tip them on the church steps. One makes one's own bunch (well, I haven't actually done it).

Two classes of bookseller. The top man is 'Tony' Carvalho, a flamboyant fellow dressed in English milord-style tweeds. He speaks perfect but somehow archaic English, 'chums' and so on. I think he must have been to an English public school in Estoril or even Brazil. Very charming and friendly.

I bought a book about childbirth, hand-coloured plates of wombs and tubes, for £150 and gave him a cheque, but when he discovered I wanted him to post it he asked me, quick as a lizard catching flies, for £4 in cash.

And on a lower level, Livraria Castro e Silva. The boss looked very like that man near Newbury who was 'hot for Maxie'.* I told him what subjects I was interested in and from a vast card index in the back room, manned or rather, womanned, by four female serfs, I was brought mounds of cards (the *Artes Decoratives* section alone about 8 inches thick).

I selected some cards and Hot-for-Maxie picked up a 1910 telephone and ordered up the books, like a waiter shouting down a tube. About twenty minutes later two boys staggered into the shop with the books. I did buy some (£182), but I was not the only customer in the shop and even paperbacks and leaflets were in the card-index.

I suspect it is something to do with living under Salazar, this obsession with cards.

In another shop I was treated like shit, until the pompous loon realised that I might buy something and I was suddenly treated like a prince, taken to the 'reserve' in fact, on the sixth floor. Mr Pompous warned me that the entrance was very low (rhyming with Slough). At last the door was opened by someone who was himself very low. I thought he was down a few steps but no, he was a hunch-backed dwarf about 2' 6'' high and not treated at all well. I fear he is paid ten pounds a week and sleeps in a jiffy bag under the table. These wonderful places have their underbellies.

Love, David

---

*One of the Cooke brothers who ran their shop from The Old Band Hut in Thatcham outside Newbury. I called there once with Howard and asked Bill if they had any books by Max Beerbohm. 'You'll have to ask Tom,' he replied, 'He's hot for Maxie.'

ROYAN, S. W. France, October 1984

Dear Howard,

What a morning! I am now on the seafront at Royan having lunch
and waiting for two antique shops to open that are said to sell
books—sent on here by a man in Saintes. It is all quite easy in
my new car.

Early this morning I called on a retired print dealer called
Maurice Tisserand. He came to the door of his bungalow behind
the station and led me down a passage (through his bathroom
door I saw the grubby candlewick cover on the lavatory seat) to an
almost empty office. We talked about old booksellers he'd known
in London in his active days. He showed me a few maps and a vast
pile of 1950s reprints of Edward Lear parrots which I have seen
from time to time, indeed my son Inigo has had to colour some
of them. Then he produced a folder of what he called Persian
Miniatures, little pages with Arabic script on one side and paintings
of tiger hunts and men with hawks on the other, and with crude
but charming borders of arabesques and flowers. I decided to buy
them. Bowling along to Saintes I thought of you and planned to
ask you what to do with them, and congratulated myself on having
branched out in this speculative way.

But just now, parking the car, I had another look at them and
concluded that they are crude, if elaborate fakes. An odd 'sixties
expression on one of the women caught my eye, and then I saw
that there seemed to be writing under the drawings. Altogether

a rather nasty feeling. It is always like that when greed interferes with one's instincts—mine had told me that someone, probably old Maurice himself, had been improving the colours, and his insistence that they had not been interfered with should have confirmed my suspicions. I seem to be constantly haunted by fear that I am being cheated these days. I was convinced that I had been conned in some way about the new car; that I'd be presented with an increase in the price and have no way of not paying up. But of course it was all in my head. Perhaps these fakes are in the head, or perhaps they are 'interesting' fakes done in Cairo in the 1880s by a well-known stallholder outside Shepheard's. At worst I can put them in cellophane pockets with 'Guaranteed Hand Painted' stickers and sell them in the Portobello Road.

Apart from this little setback I am feeling rather pleased with myself, building up a dossier of obscure bookshops against some future visit—preferably with a companion. Though when one enters a bookshop with one's mystical mantle of *confrère* and chats away (whether buying bargains or being ripped off), one is like someone coming from a storm into a haven. It is like having friends everywhere.

But it is hard to see the bookseller in Saintes as a real friend. He looked like an Oho! drawing by Rex Whistler, very thin and wiry with a face like a prune and black wire glasses.

But I must press on. I'd been relaxing over my imaginary profits, but now must make up my real losses.

David

PORTO, October 1986

Dear Howard,
Last night my room in Lisbon might have been a Vuillard. Full of furniture, a curtained window, a green iron balcony, and view of a long narrow empty street with snaking tramlines gleaming along it.

Tonight's hotel is like the set for a cheap horror movie. It is on the fifth floor and the lift opens directly into the wicked millionaire's foyer, his hard-bitten secretary sitting at a huge G-Plan desk. The windows have been disguised with heavy braid curtains and cheap Venetian blinds. There are aspidistras in big pots. The walls are dark green and hung with Old-Masterish pictures in too stingy gold frames. Beyond the desk is a wide corridor that leads to the rooms (which are very comfortable, if somewhat austere). For some reason this corridor is like a Hollywood version of the ante-room to the Grand Inquisitor's lair. Huge fake-medieval chairs with red leather seats, huge ashtrays like very tall thin bongo-drums. It is inconceivable that anyone would ever sit in here. Perhaps this place is really a brothel in the summer and only becomes a hotel in the winter when trade is slack. The maid who took me to my room fitted my bookish idea of a madam and she certainly looked rather sickened by my 50p tip.

Most of yesterday was spent with Mr Silva and his German assistant Fritz Berkmeyer, going through two whole buildings full of books.

Mr Silva clearly works on the principle that 'someone somewhere wants everything' and even in his smart shop there are twenty rooms full of carefully arranged rubbish. And round the corner in the huge 17th century palace (a pretentious brothel in the 19th century according to Fritz) the rubbish is divided into 400 sections.

Fritz told me about the many eccentric and famous dealers who had made their way here over the years. 'They come here, yes,' said Fritz in his raucous German accent, 'even if — how do you say? — we are the arsehole of Europe.'

According to Berkmeyer, one leading Lisbon bookseller often steals books. Another bookseller who had seen him slip something into his pocket said, 'What can I do? He is my best customer!'

His family have put it about that 'he is only a kleptomaniac' but Berkmeyer thinks a real kleptomaniac would not be so discriminating. One story had him at a grand wedding. During the reception he helped himself to some rare stamps from the host's library, poking them into his breast pocket along with his crimson silk hanky, later pulling out the hanky to dab his lips and causing a cloud of penny blacks to flutter into his soup.

Fritz took me to lunch in a very sordid quarter, to a sort of workman's caff. Curiously, he paused to 'put on my tie' before we left the palace. The previous day he had been delighted by my trousers. He was going to tell his wife that a famous English dealer had been to see him, 'in rags' to discourage her from nagging him about his own appearance.

I told him about the time I was visiting Hayward Cirker, the owner of Dover Publications in New York, and we discovered we had both known a con-man called Silver. 'Silver went around in his silk suit pretending to be an English gentleman, but he was just a bum from Brooklyn!' said Cirker. 'You, Mr Batterham, may look like a bum from Brooklyn but I can tell you are an English gentleman!'

After lunch we went on to a 'pub' where Mr Silva had invited us to take coffee with him. The pub was an extraordinary sort of cocktail lounge that had formerly been a haberdasher's shop and still had all the shelves and cupboards, now filled with the owner's collection of models and figures (Churchill and Hitler side by side), and terrible pastiche furniture, Harrods Art Deco style. Mr Silva, who looks like a minuscule Peter Sellers pretending to be Mr Silva, had brought his wife.

Food here is amazingly bad. If you do ever come here with me you will have to get some tips from Paul Levy. Last night I decided to eat in the hotel. I followed a dusty, carpet-walled corridor for hundreds of yards and finally came to a little Versailles-like chamber with huge chandeliers and rows of white tables. Two old men like pre-war bank managers led me to my table. The service was superb. But there was no choice. Just steamed potatoes, boiled haricot beans and an old fish nearly all bones. The potatoes and beans obviously boil and steam permanently in a room beyond Marie Antoinette's bedside screen which hides the service hatch, day after day, until a customer arrives.

In this evening's restaurant the food is just as ghastly. I even had a choice of ghastly food. I suspect the vegetables may come from a central Portuguese steamery. This restaurant does have one interesting feature: two huge washbasins with pink detergent and dirty towels actually in the dining room. Probably we are meant to wash as we leave.

When I reached the cab rank opposite my hotel this morning at 7am, all the drivers were asleep.

I woke one up but after I had got into the back he seemed to have nodded off again. But he was only praying for a moment that the car would start when he turned the key.

Toiling up one of the very steep streets, the only people I met were a boy of about six trying to pee against a wall, but hampered by a girl of four (wearing a velvet dress like an old lady) who was trying to study his parts. I grinned at them and they screamed with laughter.

Better get back to the brothel and try another 'Bulldog Drummond' story where cads and rotters really are unmitigated swine, decent chaps are White Men. Most women are decent sorts too, daughters of clergymen and retired colonels in Devon, though a few are gold-digging bitches with pasts. So far the smug narrator has confessed to the murder of three swine to help a decent sort get his girl. And one swine has murdered himself by mistake, having planned to kill a white man and then steal his wife by pretending to be her husband's best friend.

Good night, David

ALEXANDER STREET, January 1987

Dear H,

To lunch with Alan Cuthbertson, an old Australian actor in Surbiton ('opposite the tennis club'). He is one of the world's greatest experts on Rowlandson and Cruikshank. He lives in a horrid little house like an illustration in an Enid Blyton book; crazy-paving path embedded in the lawn, etc. We had lunch in the dining-room; an elaborately laid table with fish fingers and frozen peas; his loud actor's voice 'thrown' across to the pelmet and bouncing back to the hexagonal frameless mirror hanging over the fireplace. He told me how his life had been wasted, how he would really rather have had a bookshop; how he had turned down a £1,000 a week to play Malvolio. 'David, I've never really liked the part, and surely he couldn't be a man of seventy? And *then* they gave the part to Desmond Barritt and he is even older than I am!'

And he told me how David Brass of Joseph's had cheated him out of his Dickens in parts collection and how David Drummond had bought his Bécassine collection after much bargaining and then beat him down another fifty per cent after he'd had a heart attack in the shop, as a result of carrying them from Surbiton in a heavy suitcase.

And then, sitting on the bed in the spare room where he keeps his books and where he was selling me his Caran d'Ache collection (very cheaply) he said, 'When I showed this to my wife Gertrude, she looked completely blank.' He was showing me 'The cow who watched the trains go by'.

'She just rolled her head from side to side, *like* a cow, and said "What is funny about that?" I ask you, David.'

Love, David

PARIS, April 1987

Dear Howard,

I'm treating myself to a posh lunch in a restaurant called Les Bouquinistes, a stunningly restrained and elegant place, a very chic version of the old Bertorelli's. Not sure if it is old, or very new.

Really I should be treating M. Bonnefoi, my new friend. He has just paid off my anxiety about whether it is still worth coming to Paris. My last trip was initiated by his finding a set of *L'Assiette au Beurre*. Today he piled on the table an album by SEM, a set of a very rare magazine by Paul Iribe called *Le Témoin*, and other choice works which he knew I would like to buy, and I bought them. No need even to look round the shop, which is a relief because I have broken one of my three pairs of glasses, the pair I use to scan shelves.

Perhaps this restaurant is not so good. No one can eat the *plat-du-jour*, gristly bits of duck doused in pungent yellow sauce, and the potatoes are not new potatoes, as I had thought, but little balls of mashed potato fried in oil. An undignified way to kill myself. I'll stick to wine.

And now my *mousse-au-chocolat* is in a *pot-de-Limoges* five inches high, enough for eight children.

I wonder if I tried a bit harder, strolled round a few more shops and cities, I could make £1,000 every day. Without working.

Love, David

MANTES, Wednesday

Dear Howard,

Even doing nothing is pretty exhausting. The main work of the day was lunch with my old friends the Javelles in the room behind the shop. The shop doesn't shut for lunch. In fact the lunch hour is the busy time for browsers so it is very hectic. And as it is very hard to understand what my friends say, and as Claude can only shout, you can imagine it is a bit claustrophobic. But somehow very satisfying. After three hours, three bottles of wine, some porto and some obscure brandy, Jean-Marie was willing to clear the table and get out his envelope and pencil. He is very contrary or forgetful or unpredictable and his adding up is also unreliable. A stirring of entrails sort of system. For some reason Claude, who is very sharp and greedy and in charge of everything, withdrew entirely from our manly discussions. I suspect I am the only friend he is allowed. I don't interrupt or comment. Something that was £250 yesterday has gone up to £380 on the envelope, but other things were left out altogether, others grouped together and rounded down. Then the failed adding-up, the knocking-off of a discount, the tidying of digits and the drunken underlining of an acceptable bargain total. I have to pay in cash of course, opening the packet of notes pinned in bundles of ten. He enjoys this bit most of all. Much more than I do.

I feel as if I am in a novel by Balzac.

Claude's father was an auctioneer at Les Halles and Fryszman says this is why she can only shout. Her old father decided it was not a suitable trade for a girl and put her into a bookshop, Eppe's in the rue de Provence. Very soon she left her master and opened her own shop on the other side of the road, causing a row that lasts to this day, forty years on. Jean-Marie was the postman who delivered the orders from her first catalogue – and they married.

Love, David

BRUSSELS, May 1987

Dear Howard,

I saw Paul Kasmin the other evening, just off to Barcelona with Jane and Jasper Morrison and Danny Moynihan and I think Sam, though he wasn't there. Paul had just paid a world record price for a photograph by Cecil Beaton, a 'unique image' of Stephen Tennant. £3,400 sounds a lot to me. But did I hear rightly that on the back was written 'Me, waiting to be buggered'? Paul said the under-bidder was the man acting for the person he has in mind as a customer, which I thought showed enviable panache. Danny was beaming away. Presumably it was *his* £3,400.

Later

I am on my way to visit Rinus Clomp. I first heard about him in Amsterdam in about 1970 and it took me several years to track him down; eventually doing so through Arthur Minters, a dealer in NY. His 'front' is a stall on the Waterlooplein in Amsterdam on Saturdays. He gets his stock from a network of waste-paper merchants, airline hostesses and children (who buy comics from him). He has a small flat in Amsterdam but most of the time he lives in a very remote farm in Belgium near the Dutch and German border. He posts his parcels in Germany where it is cheaper and knows roads through the forest where there are no customs posts so he can do his shopping in Maastricht. His house is *inside* an old ruined wooden barn. He had it built by a retired bricklayer he met in a pub and paid in cash, at pre-war rates. His wife Frances breeds geese which she feeds on the trailer loads of stale bread that he collects from bakers shop in Amsterdam late on Saturday evenings when the market closes. "Good" books he takes home to his library, though he is happy to sell them to visiting booksellers.

I went there once with Jane and then about five years ago with Val. Frances remarked on this very sharply as soon as we arrived. 'You were with a different woman last time you were here,' and then took Val off to look at geese and complain about her lot while Rinus showed me pictures of a canoeing trip on the Dordogne where he had just been with a young woman.

'My wife doesn't like canoeing, David', he explained.

He is rather eccentric and played sentimental music on an electric organ while Frances prepared the food for us.

Back in Brussels

A difficult journey in a rented car and then again not finding the house. When I did find it the door was opened by a small child, followed by Rinus.

'You didn't know this, David, but I now have a new wife, much younger, and we have this daughter. And the reason is, my old wife died four years ago.' And that was all the explanation I got.

Anyway he seemed happier and it was his new wife's birthday and a lot of her friends came with their children.

It is quite a business to buy things because he has a terribly complicated system of cards and numbers, which means that if I make a pile of books and then look at the cards they often turn out to be too expensive to buy, and if I look at the cards and call up the books they often turn out to be not what I had imagined. In fact his accounting system is also very eccentric and I ended up with an enormous 30% discount. So I shall have to go back soon, sober and early in the day for another look.

Meanwhile I am fairly sure the coloured woodcuts by Kandinsky have comfortably covered my expenses.

I may have to give up writing you letters as I have begun to see them as a symptom of my alcoholism. Now I have gout, rheumatism and something called carpal tunnel syndrome (a sort of tennis elbow). I may have to take some action. My bag is full of pills which I never bother to take. I suffer from attacks of panic at all hours of day and night. And after 25 years as a bookseller, now even with a certain International Standing, I still have no stock to speak of and a £10,000 overdraft at the bank. And I read recently that the average man has seven pairs of trousers. I have two.

Love, David

BARCELONA, June 1987

Dear Howard,

In a review of a book by Bruce Chatwin, Camus was quoted as saying that life was a long search for what first turned one on as a child. In Bruce's case the distinctive clunking shut of an old leather-strap train door. On the move again, what exciting place is Mummy taking me to this time?

I'm not such a far-ranging traveller as Bruce but I am wondering what turned me on all those years ago. Could it not just have been a wish to get away, out, escape, and not the restless, fruitless romantic quest that Camus suggests?

In the case of my present trip to Barcelona there may be a bit of both. On an earlier visit I came across Mr Savall in a shop which is only open from 5 until 8 on Saturday evenings. A meeting which has led to a further visit to Spain.

At his house in Sarria, the Hampstead of Barcelona, he maintains a sort of *magasin privé*. A James Bond setting. A big room at the back of his house, rather like a library but slightly more like a shop, with a desk, notepads and a rubber stamp, and even a shop-front opening into an unvisited alley. Jekyll & Hyde! There was not much sign that anyone visited this place. I felt like Carter opening the tomb of Tutankamen. After an hour or so I was fetched by Mr Savall, now changed from his pyjamas into a Sunday tweeds outfit, and taken to another secret shop, even larger. He told me he would fetch me between seven and eight. It was now two! And he seemed to be locking me in, but luckily I had misunderstood him and he gave me a key. When I got back to the other house he was back in his pyjamas working in a tiny stifling room with his wife typing up my bill. £3,900. The largest I have ever seen. And also the biggest bargain I have ever found, which when joined with the second biggest bargain, from the other shop, should almost pay for the work on Val's house by the canal.

Love, David

PARIS, 2 May 1989

Dear Howard,

The charm of Paris seems to be wearing off. Or maybe my liver is wearing out. Anyway it is too hot to be driving round trying to park my huge empty car, grunting and panting as I try to back into spaces that are too small and having to drive off round a few blocks. I came here mainly to collect some books I have been waiting for since November. Some caricature albums by SEM from the Javelles.

It involved a three-hour session eating lunch and drinking too much in the cubby hole behind their shop. I usually express a sort of pride that this unusual couple should have chosen me to be their Foreign Friend. I have spent so many evenings in their flat, with their Down's Syndrome daughter Christine, the old mother, six dogs (*'les petits acrobates'* the old lady called them) and a huge telly presiding over our table. Aaron has been out to a disco with their other daughter Martine and we all went to the Robert Altman wedding when she married a farmer in Burgundy. Claude is very fat with thick ginger hair all over her face; Jean-Marie knackered by drink and working from 9 to 7.30 six days a week, even in August. And although we have been friends since 1972 I can't really understand what he says.

Claude has a flat in Trouville and another in Nice and a house near Beauvais, none of which she ever has time to visit. She is presently after a newsagent's in St Tropez which she plans to turn into a bookshop when the lease on their Paris shop runs out and the rent rises from £300 a month to £9,000. Myself, I think this figure can't be right but in all the shouting about *'milles balles'*, the rubbishing of Mitterand, cursing about taxes and prodigious anti-Semitism I've probably got confused.

Today I was inclined to wonder why, after hundreds of trips to Paris they are the only people, apart from the Fryszmans, that I have made friends with. Years ago when I came by train and took my books home with the help of porters on the boat, I sought out alarming people like Jim Haynes and once had lunch with David Hockney. I recall DH told me he had seen Vera Russell that morning and had asked her if she knew me. 'Know him!', she'd said, 'I dandled him on my knee.'*

I had supper with the Fryszmans, my other friends. I was a bit startled to find that Jacques has retired. He has suddenly become 80, having been about 65 for the past 18 years that I have known him. I was glad to hear that he has inherited Shapiro's collection of Old Master Drawings, which were always kept at his flat and should look after his old age.

I must have told you about Shapiro, probably quite a few times. He was Russian, a 'mad professor' with wild grey hair. He and Jacques and the New York art bookseller Frederick Bernett, had been contemporaries studying art history in Berlin before the war. He lived on the top floor of a huge house in Arundel Gardens with buckets catching drips in every room. He collected Old Master

---

* This was not literally true as I was six when we first met. When I mentioned this to her son Richard Burton, he told me, 'My mother never dandled anyone on her knee.'

drawings and also paintings: copies, sketches, 'afters', mostly bought in the Portobello Road in the '40s and '50s. He left his 'collection' to the Hermitage in Leningrad.

Perhaps an arrangement which allowed him to come and go to Russia himself.

When Jacques asked me to collect some books from his house I arrived to find Stephanie Maison standing on the pavement with a tally-board and men from Christie's carrying paintings out to their van. 368 of them. They were valued for probate at £1,785,000 but there was a bit of a slump by the time of the sale and after tax had been paid there were only eight pictures left. The very few the Hermitage wanted, being the most valuable, had been sold. Jacques told me today that one of the pictures sold for £250 had recently been re-appraised as a missing fragment of a Pontormo and been re-sold for £85,000.

The executors had been Stephanie Maison and a woman called Susanne Lepsius who had been Shapiro's mistress. She lived in a curious round house in the corner of a car park off Linden Gardens. She took me up when I first met her, not as a lover but to get me together with a German *protégée* of hers called Ursula. Poor Ursula. She came to England to escape from her family and worked for a firm of fur importers as a trilingual secretary. When she found she couldn't afford to live in London on her pay, the old furriers offered to buy her a flat. So she was trapped. Between them and Susanne, to whom she is enslaved, she can't escape. So she keeps a horse and rides it in Hyde Park.

Susanne has a new attendant since Shapiro died, an American: a very camp fellow with an obvious wig. He is an expert on old European royalty and a fantastically good cook. Once when I was supposed to be courting Ursula, I attended a special birthday dinner for the Prince and Princess Lieven (I think the Princess works at Christie's as an Old Master Drawings expert).

It was hard to hear all the conversations at once.

American: If the Queen of Sweden's child is a girl she will be the only woman to have Queen Victoria as a great, great, great grandmother on both sides of her family.

Princess: No, you are forgetting Igor of Romania. No! You are right! His aunt's marriage was a morganatic connection.

Prince (to Susanne): Tell me, my dear, is it true that you knew Hitler?

It turned out of course that she was not really a friend of Hitler, being only 12 in 1933. But she had been a friend of 'Lottie' Ribbentrop. And told a rather snobbish story of how the two had been sent in their Nazi *Mädchen* uniforms to 'play' with Himmler's daughter. Himmler lived in a marble palace built by Speer, and Susanne described running along corridors to find Mrs Ribbentrop and Mrs Himmler in a little overheated snug. Mrs Himmler was knitting.

Love, David

SOMEWHERE IN FRANCE, 6 May 1989

Dear Howard,

I have stumbled on one of those incredibly solid and respectable hotels that are really add-ons to their restaurants. For people who are too drunk to go home or more likely for people who book in for a week of solid eating. Perhaps that is why my room has two sinks in its salmon pink vanitory unit and a *separate* WC. I have chosen the 200F menu and have just got as far as the free course that I wasn't expecting. The beams here have a Stonehenge quality and the other diners also look very solid.

I am feeling a bit smug myself as my 'system' has been working unusually well; so perhaps I'm not the Old Wanker that some say I am; in fact I may be rather clever. I've certainly been to some very nice places. Dijon this morning, where a charming man told me that in a shop, miraculously, everything sells in the end. My own view had been a gloomier one, that a shop consists of all the books the owner has failed to sell. Of course the books I got were very cheap ; maybe they all are, there.

Midday in Beaune, a place almost too good to be true.
The bookshops here are run by couples who live over their shops and have toys on the floor.

Some special cuisine may be operating here. My *terrine* looks a bit like one of your paintings, with an orange frame and brightly coloured, obscurely phallic vegetables shining up through an amber jelly. And now they have brought a *sorbet de marc* to take away the taste.

Then on to Besançon, where there are two shops. M. George is rather pretentious, probably interested in Literature and local history; very disparaging about my requests. Clearly *he* thought I was a wanker.

'I know exactly what you want. Everyone asks for them.'

Presumably he has discouraged everyone from ever visiting Besançon again because the *other* shop was a wanker's gold mine. It looked a bit like a toy shop as the owner's collection of dolls dominated the window and the sort of customer he likes are men who spend hours looking through postcards, at last finding the one they want for the equivalent of 25p. I found piles of old *Vogue* and five boxes of a magazine I particularly like, *Le Petit Echo de la Mode* and a complete set of Oppenheimer's *Portefeuilles Mécaniques*, folio volumes on the construction of trams, submarines, mills and other machinery, with flaps which lift to reveal their workings. All very cheap and then reduced by another 25% or so as they are slapped on the pile.

David

PARIS, 29 June 1990

Dear Howard,

I've decided to make a short weekend trip to Paris to look at the fleamarkets and the Sunday bookfair. Rather absurd. It's as if I were to take a taxi to Bath and a suite at the Royal York Hotel to check out the shops in Walcot Street. Worse.

At least a taxi to Bath would take only two hours. This journey has taken 14, plus nearly an hour to find somewhere to park my car. I'd forgotten that everyone goes on holiday in the summer. The boat was a floating Piccadilly Circus of fruit machines, funny hats and dayglo shorts. I recalled the old *Maid of Kent:* no cars, First and Second Class decks, Art Deco armchairs chained to the floor in the bar to stop them all sliding to starboard as the boat had a pronounced list.

Clignancourt, lunchtime

Not a very promising start. I set my alarm for 8 o'clock, but while I was eating my *croissant* in the bar I noticed it was already 10.45. Up here in the market it is very hot, very humid and almost deserted.

Of the booksellers only Mme Denis is hanging on, her lips thinner and redder, eyes smaller and beadier, the old pretence of flirty goodwill dropped completely. Probably she'll be telling her timber merchant husband, 'Terrible day, *chéri.* Only that Mr Batterham; he's obviously gone downhill; haggard, paunchy, balding. Couldn't buy a thing. And he needs several things … shoes, trousers. *Zut!*'

Her copies of the *Gazette du Bon Ton* were £250 each. When we came to Paris for your exhibition in 1972 I bought 12 issues from Madame Arnoldy for the outrageous price of £50. At first I thought, 'If only I had kept them' – but then remembered that I had sold them to Alistair McAlpine for £250, a record price, and in theory have been doubling my money three times a year, with compound interest for the past 18 years. Hmm! Where's it all gone?

5pm

I am in a very posh *salon-de-thé* in Auteuil. Opposite the racecourse. Surrounded by smart ladies. A lot of silk and linen, little gold chains, pearls and court shoes. There is one man and I daren't look at him in case he is my Doppelganger. He's got a glazed look as if his face has been sprayed on and would crack if I tapped it. He's too tired to get up or even turn his head. His fingers are brown with nicotine and he's carrying a plastic bag from a bookshop.

It's just as well I've given up drinking. I'd probably fall off my chair and be cleared away in one of the trendy new green carts. I felt I should give up, for a while, after visiting my mother last month. After she had gone to bed I sat up very late, writing and drinking Dubonnet. I finished the bottle and then furtively took it out into the garden and hid it in the dustbin. When I came into the dining room in the morning I was appalled to see the maroon top on the sideboard. I whisked it into my pocket. Over our boiled eggs my mother said, 'It's very odd, I can't find the Dubonnet. I found the lid, but the bottle has disappeared!'

Just back from dinner with the Fryszmans. They are getting very frail; their age and weariness not helped by having to look after their seven-year-old grand-daughter who now sleeps on the same sofa in the sitting room as her mother did when I first knew them.

They had just come back from a spa in the Auvergne. But Charlotte says they are never going away again 'because of the drawings'. Old age has caused Jacques to refuse to leave his Old Master drawings behind in the flat. He'd taken them to the bank but all their large safe boxes were let out, so several hundred drawings had had to be removed from their mounts. And they are now having to be put into new mounts as Jacques found that some of the old ones were made of acidic paper and were making the edges of the drawings go brown. Charlotte is in despair. Still, he may be right to be careful. He had just forced himself to part with – I think he said four – important drawings to the Louvre, which had paid him 200,000 francs.

On my last visit we had been discussing whether collecting is an obsession, as Charlotte suspected, or a passion as Jacques insisted. Charlotte was very cheered when I said he seemed to have become more obsessive about his passion. Jacques just beamed and clearly thinks he's more passionate than ever.

Back in Alexander St.
Another 14 hour trip including the humiliation of being stopped by the Customs in the Green channel, the first time I've not gone Red for years! Nothing to declare or pay, but the full car whets their appetite.
Love, David

MADRID, 8 September 1990

Dear Howard,

Wasted the morning looking for a pair of trousers. It is very hot here and my thick grey flannels are unsuitable, particularly as I caught my pocket on a door handle stepping out of the hotel, opening a window on a strip of pallid leg.

I thought it would be simple to buy a pair of cotton bags, but there have been problems, ridicule even. I felt like H. M. Bateman's: 'The Man who Asked for Ready-Made Trousers.' Assistants with tape measures grunted at the affected difficulty of reaching round my body; others chuckled with disdain or disbelief at the cheek of my expecting to find anything that would fit me. In one shop some immense pre-war shorts were fetched from an attic. In another I was bullied into trying on something unsuitably narrow. Poncing about in front of the mirror like an old woman trying to look like a young man.

David

BARCELONA, 23 September 1990

Dear Howard,

The gout got so bad that I returned to London by the midday plane to seek medical and other comforts. A hot bath and long sleep cured the gout but all the limping had affected my back, so I still had something to grumble about. Including the new increased charges of my osteopath, particularly as the strangely soothing Mr Latey was away and I was handled by his young assistant who carelessly let slip that he would rather have been a dentist.

Arriving at the Hotel Oriente this evening was like coming home after a long voyage with too many tiring and demanding companions. The grey old gnome was at his desk and the 500 heavy brass keys on their hooks all round him. I am in Room 209, the one where the balcony incorporates the hotel monogram, over the front door.

The old lift boy has died but the lift itself is working again, the brass sliding door repaired, the frayed cables re-sellotaped. A short walk along the tiled corridor the width of your sitting room and up three steps to the 4 x 9 ft black door brought me to my room. Even *in* the room there is a corridor from the bedroom to the bathroom, a dignified modern room, circa 1910, with black and white tiles.

I am beginning to feel responsible for the Oriente's image and protective of its shortcomings. However even as a friend I have to admit the bathroom has a faintly oriental smell. This may just be because the room has been empty since August. I hope so.

[*Writing here gets a bit shaky.*]
This is absurd. The waiter here is David Methuen-Campbell. He is pretending not to recognise me because he is pissed and

wearing a ludicrous green dinner jacket with shoelace tie—but it's him alright! You *must* come here,
David

P.S. I was going back to the Oriente for a siesta. But there are so many unanswered questions. Where does one buy tinted moustache wax? Why bother to return to London?

And indeed it is a wonder that I ever did get back. My excess baggage cost £300. So I hope I've done well.

PARIS, March 1990

Dear Howard,

I've rediscovered Paris. Barcelona and Lisbon are all very well for letterwriting but there are only about five shops between them. And in any case they are both now being ruined by prosperity, pedestrian precincts, the Olympic Games and hundreds of branches of Benetton. Whereas in Paris there still seem to be hundreds of bookshops and the supply of books is volcanic. Daily sales at the Drouot, streams of runners with their green tablecloths, markets and, I suppose, frequent deaths among old book hoarders. Of course the quality of the lava is not what it was.

I remember coming here once during some economic crisis or three day week in the 'seventies. Booksellers were reacting with excessive gloom. M. Daviaud was sitting in the dark at the back of his shop grumbling that he could only take 500F out of the country. A man who has never left the 6e arrondissement.

I tried to encourage M. Parrot by suggesting that if everyone was too poor to go out to dinner or the theatre they might start buying a lot of cheap books to read. That did cheer him up. He told me that this had happened during the war. And then he added, 'Yes, and there were some good Jewish libraries coming on the market.' Sources everywhere.

In fact there are so many shops that I devised a new way of dealing with the place. One that worked last month. I gave up all idea that I should see everyone, or even a lot of shops. Instead I left my car in a car park and just wandered about, calling here and there, a bookshop here, a café there. And I found some marvellous bargains in unlikely places. M. Clavreuil for example. His distinguished shop specialises in Heraldry and Regionalism and has never seemed very promising. He is a charming man in a tweed suit like an Agatha Christie country solicitor and sits at a huge oak table. There are several assistants, pale young men in black shirts with open necks. They can be called out from windowless back rooms when lesser customers like me come in. M. Clavreuil sees to the astrakhan collar trade himself. I found a very nice book of fashion drawings and saw from the pencilled code that it had been in stock since 1981.

Love, David

Restaurant Cambuse, rue Casimir de la Vigne.

Dear Howard,

Having successfully given up drinking for the last six weeks, I had planned to give up smoking while I was here; but after finding a hotel and a place to park my car I went into a *tabac* and bought some fags and then into this restaurant and ordered a litre of wine.

This put me in a good mood. But only in the evening. In the morning I felt sad and tired. And someone had slashed one of my tyres. Possibly the Moroccan who ran the tyre shop round the corner where I had to buy a new one.

For comfort I went at once to my friends the Javelles and was invited to join them for lunch in the cupboard behind the shop; rather crowded as they already had one guest. They were in cheerful mood, revived by the death of Claude Buffet, the bookseller brother of the artist and a frequent visitor to their shop. I may have reported one of my meetings with him there years ago.

We were all gathered at the shop at the end of a day that I had spent at a bookfair. I complained that there were not enough books and too many postcards. We expounded on the absurdity of postcards and their collectors. Claude Javelle told us about a man who came every day to the shop to ask if she had any postcards of elephants. There was an odd silence and then M. Buffet asked indignantly, 'What's so funny about elephants?'

In spite of much play with plastic bottles of Badoit, I found that by 3 o'clock Alain the assistant was being sent out for a fourth bottle of wine. And as I had eaten too much of the meat loaf, which I had mistakenly thought *was* the lunch and then had to have several helpings of stewed rabbit and a mound of chips and then the cakes brought in by M. Bayard for pudding, I really felt more ready for bed than the necessary task of knocking about 60% off Jean Marie's prices.

One could say my lunch had cost about £125.

These things are relative of course. I have been wondering how I can heave myself onto a higher shelf. One of my efforts involved borrowing a huge collection of Japanese textile patterns from the shop where Luke works and trying to sell them to Terence Conran. The attempt failed of course. On the morning I called to see him the manager of Bibendum was with him and flourished a photocopy of a bill run up by a party of six the night before, for £2,315.

This dinner cost £815 more than Caroline Conran had been planning to spend on the library I am helping her to find for Bettiscombe Manor, her haunted house in Dorset. I managed to explain to her that it isn't possible to buy 1,500 Good Books for £1 each. Even at £4 it is not easy but it is tremendous fun. We go to very obscure downmarket shops and behave like big spenders, snapping up whole shelves of Dickens, Kipling, Stevenson, and a long series of early green Penguins. But it is not the answer to my wealth problem.

Love, David

BARCELONA, 19 December 1990

Dear Howard,

At last I have managed to get away again. Just before the claustrophobia of domestic life snuffed me out. No, that's rather an exaggeration. I could put it another way: before the pleasures of domesticity sapped my gambling wanderlust. Anyway, here I am.

I've been busy compiling a catalogue, as if I am shopping in my own shop. It doesn't look very interesting to me; all those unsold ceramic dogs mocking me, even in the new little coats I have dressed them in. I have to have faith in there being dog-lovers out there in Japan and Germany who will see these strays in the same light that I once saw them when I collected them.

So here I am, the Captain Foulenough of the book trade.

My new description sold three sets of *Picture Post* from my last list. It was a great satisfaction to buy back from Bernard Shapero the set I had sold him when he opened his shop in Holland Park Avenue and had failed to sell. *Vogue* is also selling well. About a month ago the phone rang and a voice, so dreary I was tempted to ring off, said 'Someone has given me your catalogue. Have you got the 1950s Vogues?' And then, 'There is only one snag. I am in Australia'.

After about half an hour's chat the dreary voice was saying, 'It looks as if you are the person I have been looking for all my life.'

Thursday. A mixed day's shopping. My best buy is a treatise with coloured photographs on sexually transmitted skin diseases.

Unsaleable of course.

And a little catalogue of socks and stockings with hairy engravings. Could be a Dada novella.

A project by a M. de Lesseps for building a canal through the Isthme de Suez 1855 is more promising. In fact I will try to make it pay for my airfare.

A small pile of 1920s hairdressing magazines is just worth having. Most reckless was a book by Eluard with woodcuts by Miró, which was suspiciously cheap.

Mr Gomez's son-in-law is more irritating and successful every visit. First he gutted the charming old shop with its 19th century wooden fittings, exposing the medieval arches, and he has now modernised it with exaggerated snowcemed pointing. He has installed a pallid linguist who now conducts all conversations, though I am still allowed to shake his hand. His prices are now so high that he doesn't speak them, he writes them on little slips of paper and pushes them across his desk. Now I hope that he has over-reached himself. He is having an exhibition of works-on-paper by a friend. All I can say is that he's a very good friend to his friend.

Little Mr Rodez has 'turned nasty' by refusing to speak English or French and insisting that I speak Catalan, which of course I can't. He's about 4ft 8ins and wears clothes made of what might have been a furnishing fabric in about 1950. He may just be in a bad mood because his wife has joined him in the shop. In fact now I think of it in this way, he *did* offer to sell me the whole shop, 'including my wife'. She and I had regarded this as his little joke.

This letter is much too long. Being a Quaker, it never occurred to my English teacher to suggest I avoid drinking while I write.
Love, David

MÂCON, 7 November 1991

Dear Howard,

I am in a very dainty hotel. Only recently converted by two lesbians from a rather drab house, like the one where Babar's friend the Old Lady lived. Everything about it is appalling apart from the owners who are delightful.

Anyway I am very glad to be here (the Balinese flute music isn't all that loud). Just had my first shower for several days. In the south of France hotel proprietors are too mean to provide soap; at least in the sort of places I stay.

I have met several interesting new cases. The booksellers seem preoccupied by how many generations of booksellers they descend from. Three of them mentioned it.

One, Mr Palliacci, a Corsican living in Nice, told me he was fifth generation, after I had shown him my guide-book which described him as '*un bouquiniste*' with '*un petit rayon de varia, cartes postales etc*'.

'I don't have good books in the shop', he laughed, 'I'd be a fool to do that. I have five warehouses so you must write to me when you come again.' To prove it he showed me into a back room. On the floor was a four-foot pile of a fashion magazine I am very keen on. He is negotiating to buy them from a woman in an old people's home in Avignon. If we all live long enough something may come of the contact.

Another fourth-generation bookseller had retired to Cannes from Lille when her first husband died. In Nice she got hold of a new one, and then when he died too she opened a shop instead of getting a third husband. A game old thing with an orange face and a lot of gold bangles. I say 'old' but now I think again, she's about my age.

The next day I went to Les Arcs where there is a bookseller called Rossignol. It is a place I have often been told about, or rather a man I have often heard about. A legendary figure respected by all other booksellers, probably in charge of the auction ring and so on, but these old boys have a softer image when they lose their teeth, and start shuffling and leaving their flies open. In fact I was not to meet him. Les Arcs is a very small place in the mountains behind Toulon. I drove through some broken gates up a leaf-covered drive and found myself on some grassy gravel in front of a wonderfully shabby but elegant 18th century wine-grower's mansion. There were several immense plane trees close to the house and the garden stretched away with broken children's swings and odd bits of sculpture, or perhaps chunks of Roman ruin.

The place looked empty and shut. I rang a bell on the flaky door panel. An upper window opened and a very old woman looked out. And came down. A wonderful woman; just the kind I always fall for. Nearer 90 than 80, I'd say, but sharp and lively and witty (well, she laughed at my jokes). Although she had a moustache she had the smile of a young girl.

When she added up the books they came to 4,380 F. I asked if I got a discount and she wrote 4,000 and then grinned and said, 'I am gaining a bit?'

On to Toulon, where I stayed in an appalling place by the sea. Utterly dead. Dozens of shut hotels and villas, shops and restaurants. My hotel, the only one open with me as its only guest, had a floodlit bamboo garden full of plastic tables, chairs and umbrellas. The best bit was opening my window in the morning and hearing the swish-swish of an old peasant sweeping the leaves.

On to Marseilles. On to Aix. On to Avignon. In Aix there were two shops. The first and worst was run by a man who looked as if he hoped I'd think he was a second son or a retired brigadier. He was wearing moccasins and a very thick pair of corduroy trousers, and his shirt hung down outside his trousers but inside his expensive cardigan. Too long grey hair and false teeth. His wife or girlfriend, also in the shop, had a foreign gypsy look: baggy suit, bangles and very red lips. The books were terrible. Rows of *Vie de Jésus* in leather bindings.

The other serious shop is very smart and expensive. The proprietor, with his moustache, erect posture and thick tweeds, looks as if he's spent many years teaching fencing at a military academy. But I think drink will crack his robust frame fairly soon. The shop does not open until 3 pm and his face was lobster-coloured when he appeared. However I bought the only book in the shop that didn't have a leather binding. A catalogue of broughams, dog-carts, Victorias and a final section on '*véhicules avec deux poneys*'. A great bargain as well as a stunning book. I may try it on the Duke of Edinburgh. 'Put it on the Duke at 5 to 1!'

George de Lucenay in Avignon was very surprised to see me. I used to visit him every year when I was driving Jo's parents to Buis les Baronnies but I have not seen him for seven years.

I know this because his daughter was only one when I was last here and had lunch with him and his wife. She comes from New Zealand and met him after visiting Avignon for a music festival. She speaks very good French and I have not forgiven her for not revealing—until I discovered it by some slip—that of course she also speaks perfectly good English. I don't think she just enjoyed seeing me struggling with my awful French; more, she wanted to pretend that she really is French.

He 'proposed' to me one of the most expensive books I have ever bought. Irresistible. An enormous album of '*calques*' (whatever they are) of the stained glass windows at Le Mans Cathedral. Very strong reds, blues, greens, orange and black. The colours reminded me of you and I wondered if you have ever done, or been asked or tempted to do, any work in stained or painted glass.

The lesbians' food is rather eccentric. A lot of chopped lemon peel in the salad. And then the dish I thought was tripe turned out to be some dainty pink pasta. Frilly knickers in a rich sauce.

I'll try the Le Mans book on the Getty Museum. It must be fantastically rare.

On tomorrow to Lyon. But I am running out of steam. And money. Val reminded me to stop buying because of having no money. And of course I won't. But other anxieties build up. Will the car pack up? Will I be robbed of all the books? What about my liver?
Love, David.

ALEXANDER STREET, December 1991

Dear Howard,

In my furtive way I've been reduced to drinking something called Lambrini which is off the bottom of any list of wines you will have come across. It is watered down to 5% and slightly fizzy.

Today I went to the shop and found it no longer stocks the stuff (no call for it in the winter). The shopkeeper, who sees me every day, did offer to get in a special supply just for me. I declined his offer.

It reminded me of the time in about 1960 when my father decided to give up smoking. He took to buying Fox's Glacier Mints. Mr Henniker got in a huge jar of Glacier Mints to feed my father's new habit. But after a couple of days my father started smoking again, so he had to buy a quarter of mints every time he passed Mr Henniker's shop on his way to the other shop in the village to buy his Weights.

Mr Henniker kept very little stock. If my mother left a list with him he had to bicycle to the other shop to 'get in' her order. After his death the shop was taken over by a Mrs Gilliard. She put up a big sign saying, 'Get it at Gilliard's.' But it was not often that my mother was tempted in. On one occasion she did go in, perhaps to buy my father some fags, and felt she should try to buy something else, so she chose a few miniature bottles which were lined up on top of the cash register.

'Stocking up for Christmas I see, Mrs Batterham,' said Mrs Gilliard.

Not much going on in the book trade!

Love, David

BEAUNE, June 1994

Dear Howard,

I like Lyon. It looks very good, like a serious town, but is more like Marshfield with its laid-back atmosphere. There are several interesting shops. M. Chartier's gets more complicated every year as he thinks up more systems to make things difficult for us. It is a huge place but he has constructed a small foyer where customers can look at a few books. Beyond this, behind him, is the vast old shop. The books are now lying on their sides, some wrapped in paper and only identifiable by a numbering system now into five figures. There is a huge old-fashioned filing cabinet with thousands of cards each covering a different subject. The files are brought out to the cubby-hole where customers rack their brains. Worse still, the prices are written in a code of letters and numbers which have to be checked against a list stuck on the wall.

M. Miraglia is more straightforward. His books are sitting there on their Remploy shelving. I wish I could buy the 15-volume surgical atlas with its stunning coloured plates for £5,000 or the vast birds-eye view of 18th century Paris for £2,500. Or even the eight volumes of coloured plates of toadstools for £1,800. They all seem rather good value but I have avoided collecting any customers rich enough to benefit from having me as a supplier. Of course it would make more sense. They are the same kind of thing that I normally deal in, just more expensive. Oh well!

Across the river in the old town, now rather ruined by pedestrian precincts and bollards, I had a very satisfying experience. Just after I arrived in the shop another bookseller came in and asked about magazines and was shown a pile of *La Chasse Illustrée* which I had not noticed.

I told M. Diogène in an aside that, if the other bookseller didn't take them, I would. A few minutes later I was quite shocked when the man said he'd like to buy them and M. Diogène told him they were already sold to me. I hurried into the back room in case there was a row but the poor fellow sloped off.

Love, David

PARIS, 1994
In Le Petit Saint Benoit restaurant

Dear Howard,

It is twenty-one years since your exhibition in the rue de Seine,
when I was brought here first. Must be *ten* years since we came
here together and we drank so much that you fell asleep on the
bus to the wrong airport.

Not sure if it was Man Ray or Max Ernst who held court in this
café on the Place Saint Sulpice. He lived across the square behind
my hotel. When he died, whoever it was, his house was found to
be full of money, most of it no longer valid, hidden in drawers,
behind pictures, in teapots, behind the cistern. Not much chance
of that happening when I die. I've been brooding a bit, plodding
round the shops, on how it can be that after all these years at
my trade I am so much worse off than I was to start with! It's
probably because I am more interested in the booksellers than
in the wheeling and dealing.

In the rue de Seine I surprised a very elegant woman trying
to park her car; a few minutes later she was across the street as
I passed the Galerie Claude Bernard. By now she was wearing a
ludicrously expensive-looking coat and swinging her handbag
down near the gutter on a gold chain. I think she thought I was
following her.

I decided she was on her way to meet a lover. She darted into
the hotel where Oscar Wilde died. It has been done up in such a

grand way that the rooms start at 1800F, according to a card in the window. No hourly rate given.

Mr Garnier Arnoul, a very old dealer in theatrical books has moved into a new shop. New shelves, new floor, new door. I asked him what had happened to Didier Terroy, his former assistant, who used to run books to me in Alexander Street when weekending with a friend in the Portobello Road.

'*Il est mort … mangé par un crocodile au Cameroun …* '

Next day

I am trying to arrange that the habit of not drinking becomes as compelling as the old habit of drinking too much.

Looking round – not just the underbelly of the French book trade but the *refusés* of the antique trade too – where I now am, there is hardly anyone whose face is not puce, hands puffed and stiff, eyes glazed with rage or disappointment. Perhaps not surprising when one sees the tons of rubbish they have brought here from all over France and will be humping back again in ten days' time.

p.m.

Back with Man Ray's ghost. Back from supper with the Fryszmans. One of Jacques's worries is how to get rid of all his books in case he dies. So far he is only giving a 50% discount on everything he still has, so I bought a few bargains.

Love, David

HEATHROW, 26 June 1995

Dear Howard,

An unusually high level of anxiety brought me here two hours early. But better than three hours late as I was on my last visit to Finland in 1962 when I was a wallpaper merchant. At the Cromwell Road terminal I found I had left my passport at home. My taxi back to Blackheath and then on to the airport ran out of petrol. (The fare was £4 I remember!) And I was wearing thick vests in anticipation of the Finnish cold. Phew!

When I finally arrived at Helsinki airport, a furtive group of huts covered in snow in a forest clearing, I found that I should have had a vaccination certificate. I was led away by a woman in a white coat to the inoculation hut. As I lay shirtless on a bed waiting for the needle, a crackling Tannoy was fatuously calling my name. Three managing directors had been waiting six hours for me in the bar but somehow they managed to get me to the station and onto the night train to Tampere.

The train owed nothing to Aalto or Tapio Wirkkala. It was the sort of train that brought Russian Matisse collectors to Paris at the turn of the century with velvet seats, tasselled gas-lamps, Art-Nouveau carving. I fell in with a man who spoke eleven languages, including Latin, or so he said. He offered me two bits of advice which he said were essential for visitors to Finland. The first was that if I saw something that reminded me of Russia—a woman driving a steamroller perhaps—I should say nothing about it. The second thing that I should understand was that when one takes a drink with someone one must catch their eye and in formal situations hold it as one drinks.

It was useful advice. The next time I met the managing directors, in another bar, they ogled me in a way I might otherwise have found disturbing. And when later they drove me on a tour of the town and we passed through a bit of 17th century Russia with an onion-domed church and priests with black beards and birettas hurrying in and out, they made no comment and neither did I.

HELSINKI, 27 June

The Old Russian Square is nowhere to be found. Perhaps I invented the 'memory' to go with the story or it may have been pulled down. There is a huge area in the centre of town which has been cleared, flattened. I did go to the Russian Orthodox Church. I liked the huge sign saying NO SHORTS.

I have been to ten of the thirteen shops. I have found a very beautiful, very expensive Russian book about horses It is £550. I shall have to buy it and try to sell it for £1,200 to pay for this visit.

I have bought the Russian book. Perhaps the Duke of Edinburgh will buy it, to sell to someone who wants to give him a present. Did I tell you this curious fact about the Royal finances which I have discovered? The Duke keeps a cupboard of goodies, such as the books he buys from me, so that people who want to give him a present can choose something he is known to like! They then buy it from him and give it back.*

Sunday morning
I am sitting in the Café Ursula overlooking the harbour, watching great floating hotels coming and going, from Sweden and Russia. And I've just come across a curious place not mentioned in the guidebooks: a series of wooden pontoons, each with six wooden tables where people can bring their rugs and carpets to scrub them with buckets of water. There is a giant municipal mangle and a row of rails where the carpets are hung out to dry. The equivalent of washing the car on Sundays, I suppose.
Love, David

* The Duke was a good customer for a while. I didn't meet him myself but dealt with him through his private secretary. At our last meeting he told me, 'I will show these to Prince Philip but I doubt if he will be able to buy them. I happen to know he is rather strapped for cash at present.'

SOMEWHERE IN FRANCE, July 1997

Dear Howard,
Coming up the motorway from Toulouse I gave a lift to a bizarre Englishman.

I am not sure if he was an ordinary madman, let out for a few days, or a Chatwin-type madman. A minor-public-school type with a stagey military air, a rather too large moustache (I thought) and something of boot-polish about his hair. He said he was in the Spanish Foreign Legion in Morocco. Can there be such a thing? A monastic outfit where the men sleep in vast dormitories on three-tier bunks. But not quite like a monastery as the regiment had its own brothel. Three brothels in fact. For Officers, NCOs and Men. Hang on a minute! Surely they couldn't have recruited 750 women from convicted prostitutes in Spain and offered them work in lieu of a prison sentence? And even in the Foreign Legion could visits to a brothel three times a month really be compulsory? And why was this loon spending his first leave in five years on what he called a 'survival test' on the French motorway system, on which, he pointed out, one can eat, sleep and work? Perhaps I was supposed to slip him a fiver.

Reached Bollmeir's shop in Bergerac in the late morning. He was wearing a thick white roll-neck pullover and as his very long crinkly hair hung down all round his head, including the front, he looked rather like an exotic plant sitting at his desk.

He has a sweet nature and calls his mother frequently and became very worried when I suggested lunch because he had to check on his parents at midday. Near the shop, down by the river, he has bought a huge 17th century townhouse where he hopes one day to live and move his business. A very long job, I think. Nearly every room is in the middle of some process or crisis: plastic sheeting everywhere, the stench of Cuprinol, every kind of rot being progressively revealed as the restoration advances. Next to the house is a huge corrugated iron shed, once a working garage and on the site of what had originally been the walled garden of the house and that he now plans to reinstate.

I spent £800 on solid, double-my-money old favourites.
David

PARIS, 24 October 1997

Dear Howard,
I am in the Hotel Récamier again. In the Place Saint-Sulpice. It is like coming in and out of an etching, in about 1910. In the corner, with a few trees, a light in the window, a tramp arranging his bags on a bench.

Have spent more money than I usually do. I keep forgetting that one is supposed to offer half what one is asked. On the other hand my new friend Nicole was so keen to sell me another set of *L'Assiette au Beurre* that she told me to take it away and pay for it in cash when I return. I like it when people do that; it makes me feel that I have 'arrived'.

Friday
To dinner with the Fryszmans, now very shaky. Jacques told a story of his return from prisoner of war camp on VE Day, May 8th 1945, which was also his birthday and the day on which he was miraculously reunited with his brother Max. The returnees were

sent to The Rex cinema in Paris. Jacques said that some people had to sleep in the cinema but that others were welcomed in some way by local residents and released early. A 'charming young lady' whose father had a hotel opposite the cinema had invited Jacques and he did not have to sleep at the cinema.

Just then Charlotte interrupted, 'You *never* told me that before, Jacques!'

He also showed me a notebook he had compiled when a prisoner, with little drawings of his companions and messages from them in Russian, Turkish, English and other languages. 'Nearly all of them must be dead by now', he said.

Next he got out some photographs of his grandparents and I managed to change the subject.

Next day

Into a Russian bookshop in a courtyard. Run by a very charming man. The kind of man I'd like to be myself if I could arrange it. Couldn't buy anything of course.

'I suppose these kinds of things are "*introuvable?*"' I asked him. '*Introuvable!*' he beamed as if I'd just given him a large cheque.

While I was there an enormous man came in. Very tall, 60 inch chest, 90 inch waist, Roman head, shaggy eyebrows and long grey hair. He handed over a large folded paper. The proprietor took it in silence and then wrote a long message in Russian, in capital letters with a red felt pen. The giant folded the paper into his double-breasted jacket and left again without a word.

A Romanov valet perhaps, who took a vow of silence after the death of the Czar?

Then in a street where I had never been before I saw a shop which had clearly just opened. A very smart print and map shop with shelves of large green portfolios. One wall had books on glass shelves. Miró, Picasso, Bonnard and Co, in fine condition in their dust jackets. Prices always in multiples of 500 francs in this kind of shop.

A woman in green silk with an orange face tensed as I came in tieless and carrying a plastic bag. But out on the pavement, lounging, was a man who seemed vaguely familiar. He was the only other bookseller invited to the Javelle wedding and had now left his old employers in the rue Peletier and started on his own. He has the pleasant air of a man who makes plenty of money without taking things too seriously.

He led me through a maze of alleys and courtyards. Fifty yards beyond the front door of a shop in the rue Mazarin and then through another iron door was a huge room, an Aladdin's cave of shelves and piles. It was clearly not the done thing for me to rummage but my host dug away in a corner and came up with 15 volumes of *La Mode Illustrée*, bound with all the folding dress patterns. Just the kind of thing I like. 'These all lack the coloured plates', he explained and suggested a price that would give me £1,500 profit. Back in his parlour I spent the £1,500 on a run of *Le Manuel du Peintres en Bâtiments*, a professional decorating magazine made up of coloured plates of marbling, *faux-bois* and three-dimensional typefaces.

Love, David

SOMEWHERE IN THE DORDOGNE, 3 February 1998

Dear Howard,

I went to Paris on Sunday, taking in a bookfair in the afternoon and then came on to Toulouse by Motorail and *couchette*. I felt very adventurous. But at 7 am in Toulouse, with a hangover, things looked bleak and then the shop that is supposed to be open on Mondays was closed …

Luckily I found a lot of books after lunch and recovered my normal illusion of activity and optimism. French provincial booksellers are either reserved and scholarly or they are oddly raffish, more like fairground or circus folk. They often have long hair worn in a bun like my man this afternoon.

Next day

After last night's dosshouse this place is a paradise. The Auberge de la Reine qui Chante is the setting for a film by Chabrol with a script worked on by Simenon *and* Agatha Christie.

It is very pretentious in a seedy 1930s-ish sort of way but has probably been ruined by the new motorway which hums not far away.

An elderly battleaxe runs it. There is a huge padded menu, like the programme for a gala performance, with meals from 55F to 230F, any of which can be concocted in a few minutes by an old drunk behind a hatch across the hall.

The hotel is '*complet*', Myself, a handsome black man with a vintage Mercedes, a young woman who is leaving at 6.30 in the morning, and a man who says he is the manager of an abattoir and seems to have left now to go to work. There are no other guests in the restaurant which has places for about sixty. There is a waiter, about 14, not bright but keen, in a starched white jacket.

If the plot thickens I'll let you know ... but probably Simenon and Christie didn't hit it off and I've been dropped, won't be developed ...

Love, David

MADRID, May 1998

Dear Howard,

I find it difficult to write letters now that I have given up drinking. It is impossible to recapture that feeling that I was being amusing, interesting, affectionate. And, of course, seeing the situation as it is now, it is alarming to contemplate what may have been churned out, under the influence, in years past.

It is even tempting to blame the poor state of my business on lack of alcohol (except that, looking round Alexander Street, there are as many mistakes left lying as there may have been rash purchases sold in the past). Certainly my 'system' has stopped working: those short relentless forays, sweeping up unsaleable books that only I seemed to have found a market for.

I got here yesterday and found that, having failed to make the obvious enquiries, there is a big book fair here in two days' time, when I intended to be in Barcelona. Also, most of the shops in Madrid are shut; they are humping their rotten stock to the street where the fair will be for the next two weeks.

Luckily Val pointed out that in the scale of disasters, having to spend a day in Madrid is not high on the list and, although the night was plagued by fears, I set out cheerfully in the morning and was soon reminded of aspects of foreignness that I relish. First an enormous black bag lady asleep in a niche in the Gran Via. Black bag ladies must be 'very rare', 'scarce' at least. And then I went into a church; a hole-in-the wall sort of place on the outside but full of action within. Gilded saints, bleeding hearts, candles (including banks of electric ones that light up when money is paid over). In one corner there was a glass box in which a marble figure of Christ brought down from the Cross was lying. His head was resting on a real lace pillow. His feet extended through a hole in the glass box and a young man was grasping them both with his two hands, swaying and rocking as if on a pinball machine. He looked a bit like Inigo and was clearly in desperate need of divine help.

A long walk through little nineteenth-century streets where no tourists need to go, took me past wonderful old shop-fronts — perfumery, buttons, cheese, laundries — hardly bigger than cupboards and with almost no stock. My bookshop was here; bigger than a cupboard but with no stock at all. Just a very old man waiting to sell the building, if he lives, and, rather oddly, doing a bit of mending as he waits.

Then I walked miles to another bookshop. As I got near, I could see, far off, a big hand-painted sign saying 'Bookshop for Sale', but it was still open and after a lot of chatting I bought a copy of a book I love called *Les Meilleurs Blés*, a seed catalogue with coloured lithographs of ears of corn. The old man trebled the price when I said I wanted to buy it, but luckily his daughter halved his price when he wasn't looking.

At lunch an old Swede at the next table complained that he could not hear Swedish radio in Spain. His daughter is the presenter of a classical music programme that signs off each midnight with her saying, 'This is Bo Lindstrom wishing you sweet dreams.' He has a tape of this with him, but apparently it's not the same.

Love, David

PARIS, 26 October 1999

Dear Howard,

I'm feeling very sorry for myself. Running, as I thought, to prevent my car from being towed away from outside the backdoor of the Théâtre Odéon, I fell in the street. One person collected my glasses, another my book and newspaper, and a third heaved me to my feet, saying 'You must be careful, old Sir.' I felt like someone in a Babar book. Also as if my leg had snapped off. Soon I realised I needn't call an ambulance, but I did try to buy some crutches. Had to settle for strong painkillers.

David

ALEXANDER STREET, December 1999

Dear Howard,

I loved my visit to your French house but I nearly didn't make it. I've been feeling so seedy lately that even when I had reached Le Touquet I felt it might be politer to ring up and make some excuse rather than inflict myself on you when shaking with ague and full of self-pity.

All that faded when I reached the village. The Butcher came out of his shop to give me directions: 'When you leave the town, take the Fork to the right. Go through the Forest. You will come to a Cross. There you must turn right and continue until you see the Castle in a Circle of Trees. Good luck!'

And then, there were all the lights (and the *gardien's* Christmas tree winking sadly at his telly). As I approached the arch I thought for a moment there was a lowered portcullis. I wondered if there would be a bell on a chain or if hounds would appear.

And then looking into the kitchen window and seeing you all there among the pans and food and lights another scene from Grimm or Perrault.

Of course one obvious source of happiness in your house is the luxurious warmth. When I visited country houses in Scotland in the 1950s people *boasted* about the overcoats they had to wear on the walk from the drawing room to the dining-room, where they would be flung on a steaming heap like a dung-hill in the corner.

I am sorry I didn't say a proper goodbye but it was as well that I left very early. It took some time to get the ice off my windscreen and, when I did get going, I could have done with a man with a torch to lead me through the mist, even the first few miles to the motorway. Antony's instructions had ended, 'Have 4 Euros ready for the toll,' and since I had no change I was worried almost as far as Calais that I would come on some unmanned barrier and be trapped!

David

ALEXANDER STREET, 3 January 2000

Dear Howard,

The snow has melted. It's raining. All the parking places are still empty. The postman has just delivered two adverts. Thomas is still in France, we suppose.

We spent the New Year with Andy and Polly in Somerset, partly to stay as far away as possible from fireworks for the sake of our old dog Rocky who hates them.

We did take part in one Millennium ceremony. Seamus Heaney had long planned to be at Thomas Hardy's childhood church at Stinsford on the eve of the century as Hardy himself had been a hundred years ago, and to read the poet's 'The Darkling Thrush'.

Seamus and Marie flew over to Bristol and after lunch we went in two cars to Stinsford on the edge of Dorchester. I caused a ripple of unease by suggesting that there might be crowds of Hardy Society members (from Australia, South America, etc.) with the same idea. But if there were, they had all left by the time we arrived in the pouring rain and huddled under a yew tree by Hardy's grave.

It seemed like a very good way to have spent the afternoon, when we got back for our tea. It made me think of my dead friend Giles Wordsworth and how much he would have liked to be with us, serious Hardy buff and snob as he was in equal measure. I can hardly qualify as a Hardy expert but I do relish having been part of this moving little fancy!

Happy New Year, David

PARIS, October 2003

Dear Howard,

We arrived too late in Paris for me to face visiting the bookfair at the Porte de Champerret. Each year the 'dealers days' get earlier and had now slipped back to the day-before-the-day-before the opening day. I have 5000 Euros spread about my many pockets; 1000 in an envelope to give to Nicole Leclerc if I see her.

Next day. After several hours at the fair I have spent 700 Euros. William Nicholson's *London Types* and some men's fashion plates from the 1930s: rotters in suits, often with cigarettes hanging from limp wrists or grim lips.

No sign of any other English dealers and several familiar Frenchmen no longer present.

I found Nicole. It seems she has sold her business to one of her former employees. She had lost weight, bought new clothes, and looked much happier—it occurred to me she might be 'on' something—and came alarmingly close when I gave her the money.

We had lunch in the Moroccan café near the Place de Champerret. The same skull-headed waiter is there, twenty years on. Val was impressed that he knew I would ask for a cheese omelette and half a bottle of Badoit.

In the evening I made some notes about what we had spent and added up the money I had left in my pockets. One pocket was empty. 1000 Euros were missing!

As Val had given me several lectures about having so much money on me, I couldn't share this disaster with her. She had even offered to lend me her money belt, a sort of one-breast bra, with straps and a zip.

My guilty secret made me behave as if in some deep depression, certainly 'not much fun to be with'.

Next day, after visiting only one bookshop we left town and headed for Amiens. After several missed turnings and directions from people who knew no more than we did, we arrived at the Amiens branch of Emmaüs. The Communauté Emmaüs is a combination of monastic order and jumble sale. Down-and-outs and dried-out alcoholics live communally. They earn their keep by recycling rubbish donated by local people, and then selling it back to other local people on certain afternoons.

On these days do-gooders, known as the *responsables*, arrive to supervise the selling of the rubbish, and handle the money. A parade-ground-sized shed houses the furniture: aisles of neatly arranged wardrobes, beds, tables and three-piece suites; a further section curtained off with plastic sheets is the knacker's yard where this furniture is finally chopped up into bundles of kindling after the prescribed number of months on offer. There are more spaces like indoor tennis courts where the *responsables* sell the books, the clothes, bric-a-brac, and *bibelots*.

The *bibelot* section is where Val stocks up on rosaries and crucifixes. Until recently she was selling these in bulk to Gilbert & George from her stall in Spitalfields Market. But now they seem to have enough. Enough for what? We shall see.

I try not to buy anything but I am sometimes tempted by needlework-by-numbers pictures, a Manet or Frans Hals. This trip I turned down two identical Vermeers.

By the time we left the shed it was too late to visit the very dull bookshop and we pressed on to Gravelines.

In England Gravelines is associated with the huge nuclear power station polluting the Channel. But the town itself is charming, the nearest bit of Abroad. It is dominated by a fortress built by Vauban and there are miles of moats and ramparts with paths and little green places.

While we were sitting over our *moules marinières* in the evening Val suddenly said, 'This money belt is rather scratchy. Now we are out of Paris I think you should look after this cash yourself.'

I still didn't like to admit that I'd lost the money but I did cheer up. Visibly. Val said later that she thought this was because of the tiny *pichet* of wine I had ordered. And had thought, if David is so hooked on wine that it has this marvellous effect on him, I must give up trying to get him to cut down on the booze.

P.S. I went to Ben John's memorial lunch at the Chelsea Arts Club. Several people gave speeches about aspects of his life. The common theme seemed to be how stingy he was, though he was good at pretending this was just his little joke.

I reported this event to my brother. To my surprise he reminded me how tiresome we had found Ben in Cornwall during the war and how we used 'to cut up through Duck Street' to avoid meeting him.

And he also remembered how when Mrs Cornish used to complain about Ben, her husband Jim told her, 'They are all good boys.' I cried when I read this. And I'm crying now. Not sure why!
David

ISTANBUL, May 2002

Dear Howard,
I am not sure if I am a deviant or a pervert.

I have never been able to do it without thinking of someone. Now I find it difficult to do it at all, even if I can think of someone. And I used to hope I'd get better at it and perhaps spread myself about a bit.

I am talking about letterwriting, of course, and I dare say you half expected at least a postcard as I am in Istanbul.

This is our last day and I can't help thinking we have done those things that we ought not to have done and left undone those things which we ought to have done. It depends on who one listens to:

Tony Neville (bookseller): Never been there. I hate Turks, you see. They are all crooks.
Tony Seaton (travel historian): Apart from a few palaces Istanbul is rather like Birmingham.
Lois St Pierre (archaeologist): There are so many layers of history. It's a comfort to know the Hippodrome Hotel is only a few hours

away if I need to get away from London. And there are lots of bookshops.

Bernard Shapero (bookseller) : There are no bookshops.

Turkish spellings create an illusion of childlike simplicity which diverts us from what is going on inside their prisons. On the balcony of the Aya Sofia I saw marks scratched on a marble balustrade, and next to this a printed sign, VIKINGS GRAFFITIES IS ILLEGIBLES.

The menu in our hotel, an elaborate printed job, has a section, 'From the Gills'. And was it perhaps a double shot of Turkish wit that made the souvenir shop at the Galata Tower put up a sign, Im' SORRIE, WE ARE OPEN?

I think I am too far gone to get deeply into mosques but I can still get a buzz from crocodiles of schoolgirls. They wear tartan skirts with white or blue stockings and shirts buttoned up to the chin. In the Topkapi Palace garden I even saw some cubs and guides, with caps, badges, neckerchiefs and toggles. Their akela was wearing a Burberry scarf.

Near the Rüstem Pasha Mosque is a very narrow street where the old secondhand shoe market is still going. Stocks much thinner than in the carpet bazaar. Some merchants only had three pairs. Thomas thought they might be getting their stock from outside the Mosque. Perhaps even some form of Islamic charity operates here, buying back one's stolen property from the poor.

I have been to a few bookshops. Only two detained me for more than a moment. One was the English Bookshop in a basement along the street from our hotel. Very bare and tidy, looking as much like a video shop as the owner could manage. He invited me to sit down and asked if I could find him thousands of cheap Penguins.

I said I could and then asked if there were any serious old bookshops. There is the Librairie de Pera. I am going there tomorrow. It is closed today. It doesn't look like a shop that arranges auctions. All the windows on the first floor are broken.

But it may be as good, or better, than my other shop that was in the book section of the Grand Bazaar. A tiny cupboard-like place, very neat. A quick glance showed me it was as dud as all the others; but then I spotted a copy of Séguy's *Papillons*, one of the rarest and best *pochoir* portfolios, leaning against the back wall. This was 'Ming vase in an Oxfam shop' stuff. I took it down expecting the man to say $2,000 or $10,000. The price was $200. This made me sure it must be a cunning Turkish reprint. But Val pointed out that even a Turk would not be cunning enough to remove a few pages and cut out one or two butterflies to make it look better. But I am still suspicious.

Dinner time
On the menu was CROBS — something caught in or near Istanbul? My companion had the RAVIOLLI.

On the aeroplane. Phew!
A wonderful but wasted morning. I walked up past the Topkapi and down the little street of restored houses which is now an

expensive hotel with authentic decor, including ottomans, sofas, divans and poufs in all rooms. Kasmin told me about it and will be there himself on the 2nd of May.

At the foot of the lane I caught the tram down to the Galata Bridge. I walked across the Golden Horn! The sun sparkling on the water. Ferries coming and going like patterned water beetles with their rows of orange lifebelts. Appalling traffic. Frightful fumes. A long section where the pavement was blocked off completely. From the end of the bridge I found the Tünel, a funicular railway built in 1885, the mosaic ticket office now very shabby. From the top of the Tunel it was a short walk to the Librairie de Pera and perhaps to the Pera Palace but I couldn't find it.

Mr Ooms had not arrived. Nearly all the shops in the street sold musical instruments. His neighbour said he usually arrived at nine. Half an hour later his other neighbour said, 'Half an hour. Maybe more.'

By now I was part of the landscape. A man came out of a cake shop and warned me not to stand where I was. He pointed to a crumbling parapet above my head, 'Dangerous!'

I tried another neighbour. 'Maybe ten?' he suggested, smiling.

A man fiddling with an electrical gadget on the wall asked me to come into his shop for a free coffee. It was a coffee shop. Down some steps there was a room about 8ft square with a gas ring and pots for making Turkish coffee and tea. There were also some tiny tables and chairs, the right size for a Teddy Bears Picnic. My host introduced me to another man, 'This is my Big Brother.' I managed to get down onto one of the Teddy's chairs and Big Brother made me some coffee.

They checked from time to time to see if Mr Ooms had arrived.

All the while a little boy hurried in and out with a swinging tray. Out with a tea or coffee and then, he threw each time he came in, a very small coin into a jar on the counter,

I managed to get back onto the street with much smiling and hand-shaking and refusal of the tiny coins I offered. I had been puzzled how the orders for the drinks were taken. I now saw that the gadget I'd seen my host fiddling with was a sort of baby-alarm of which there were several hanging along Music Street.

Mr Ooms never turned up but by then I began to feel like Isaac Bashevis Singer, spying on my neighbours, not for profit but to put them in my letter.

Love, David

NICE, a late breakfast in the station, April 2004

Dear Howard,

Not a good start. I stumbled from my *couchette* after 12 hours fitful sleep and bad dreams and found I had left my washbag and razor in my car. I paid an underground *concièrge* for the use of a '*cabinet de toilette*', a minute cubicle with no plug in the basin. A sign on the back of the door said '*Limite 20 mins*' – Double charge after that.

And then as I bustled in here for my free breakfast, trying to look businesslike, two legs of my chair slipped off an unseen ledge and I fell to the floor.

Stayed the night with my cousin in Grenoble. And on to Lyon. Thin pickings. Desperate, I bought some very expensive trade catalogues from the maddening M. Benharbon who has all the best books. Now I am studying the *Album de Chaussures l904* and I feel quite uneasy at being seen looking at it. Have you ever seen a pair (well, a single, here) of *'Balmoral Franco-Américaine'* or *'Bottines Officiers (Elastiques)?'* Gleaming black patent leather, with highlights, holland inserts, buttons and flaps — Proustian rotter stuff. But these are just the shoes the fetishists wear themselves. Part II, *'Chaussures pour dames'* is unashamedly kinky: *'Bottes lacées pour la chasse'* and *'Fantaisie Américaine.'*

Beaune

The bookseller here reminds me of myself in some way — a self I am trying to disown but which might reappear if I decided to have a shop. Fair Isle jersey, keen on reading, kind to old ladies; arranges the window very prettily and sits in the snug back room mounting pictures torn from books.

Love, David

Dear Howard,

It is not a good time of year to be in Barcelona. Too hot and humid but worst of all are the huge number of tourists. Great crowds young and old swirl through the streets like starlings looking for a place to roost. Every café in town has spilled onto the pavements with tables and chairs. The Ramblas has a row of tented restaurants bustling with waiters in different coloured shirts, like a beach in Saint Tropez.

To cope with all the visitors, dinner is served all day and not just after 10 pm. The menus consist of big plastic folders with photos of the food on offer, Bacon and Eggs, Hamburgers, and so on.

This morning however I am Up Town. No tourists here. I am on the street, but the *menú del día* is written on a blackboard in Catalan. I have no idea what I am ordering but I am too proud to admit this. This has always been a foible of mine.

Once in Madrid I strayed into a very old and famous restaurant, all fake medieval woodwork and velvet drapes. The other customers were huge Franco fans accompanied by their big wives. I studied the menu and ordered something by pointing with my finger. After a long wait three men in white coats came to my table with a trolley which they manoeuvred into position by my side. At a signal one of the men moved a small dish from the trolley to my plate. A second man began stirring the little pot with a wooden spoon, and the third man lit a match causing a blast of bluish flames which gradually sank down and eventually went out. The three men clicked their heels and withdrew, backwards, taking their trolley and leaving me with my midget's delight. The dish was elvers, surely illegal everywhere else? I can't remember if they tasted of anything.

In England we wear our belts below the paunch. Here in Up Town Barcelona the fashion is to wear the belt above the paunch, often causing an unpleasant creasing near the crotch. Pale brown is this year's colour for trousers and jaundice yellow short-sleeved shirts to tuck into the over-paunch belt.

I am waiting for a shop to open.

In Madrid, near the Prado, there is a little street of bookstalls, very charming, faintly Russian-looking, with fretwork eaves.

In Barcelona there is a similar street near the university. But the cabins provided by the council are more like those temporary offices or lavatories used by builders. Metal boxes on stubby legs. I always come here because I once found some very good toy catalogues here.

Most of the cabins are closed today, as if the owners had died and no one bothered to mention it. The only one that is active is attended by a man on crutches. The inside of the little shop is so full that he can no longer get inside himself and is standing out on the pavement. The only books visible are on the fold-down flap. Mostly porn magazines. I hope you didn't already know that there is a magazine called *Fist Fuck*.

Love, David

PARIS, 2004, Hotel Recamier

Dear Howard,

I arrived at the *Marché aux Vieux-Papiers* yesterday and found that I had come on the wrong day. No sign of life. Perhaps it will be tomorrow.

And when I got to Dover yesterday the passport I flourished turned out to be Val's; but luckily my bus pass did just as well.

And then last night I had a meeting with a bookseller at his house in the Place Monge. He gave me a code to access the building. Nobody there! After half an hour I called him. He was there but I had not realised that tapping in the code would have opened the massive front door if I had given it a massive shove.

I managed to reach M. Santon in the Passage Jouffroy and give him the 2,200 Euros that I had owed him for over a year, but he immediately got out a key, turned out the customers in his shop, including me, and set off to the auction room nearby.

But it is a very nice day and I am here at a café on the pavement. I keep catching the eye of a man across the aisle. He looks rather familiar; perhaps a bookseller from the past. But he may be Donald Sutherland. He was Mr Bennett in the film of *Pride and Prejudice* last time I saw him.

I am having a *café liégeois* for my pudding. The first time I had one was at Aux Lyonnais, a restaurant where we all dined after your exhibition in the rue de Seine in 1972. There were also inedible meringues I remember; we signed them as one might a cast on a broken arm and took them home as souvenirs.

Living in the past again! In those days I could have walked from here to a lot of bookshops that are no longer open: M. Rouam, M. Vivien, M. Davioud, Mme. Arnoldy, M. Colas and his uncle old M. Colas (who looked like Charlton Heston), Michel Roethel, Librairie du Cygne, M. Gallant, Librairie Visconti. All gone.
Love, David

ALEXANDER STREET, April 2005

Dear Howard,
The Smithfield fair was more fun than the Russell Hotel book fair, but after taking only £79 for a ten-hour shift, seeing you and Antony was definitely the highlight of the day.

The old man in the doorway of a shop opposite my stall can never have been a highlight but he put on a good show. When he arrived he was dressed as Father Christmas with a badly fitting beard and a false nose. I was glad there were no children about. Val said he looked like someone from a Stephen King horror novel.

The next time I noticed him he had removed the red costume, a top layer, and was dressed in camouflage fatigues. After fumbling in his several carrier bags he produced a frilly paper hat in the shape of a St George's cross and fitted himself with a St George's flag cape. Hardly worth a second look this month, so he was soon out of that and wearing a huge felt hat with Guinness written on it and a pair of clown-size pink glasses ten inches across.

A tourist going by stopped to take a photograph of him. He obviously thought this would earn him a tip but the photographer passed on not realising the man was 'working'.

I felt rather sorry for him and also curious, so I went across to talk to him. I gave him a pound which he palmed with no hint of obsequiousness or gratitude. Looking up at me with a toothless Goyaesque face he confided, 'I am a millionaire, you know.'

'Where do you keep your money?'

'In a bank. I can't carry it about. I'd be mugged … They take my bags. They even took my chair!' he explained.

Later he was back in his Father Christmas outfit and I heard him talking to another local man. 'I haven't had a cigarette all day. No one seems to smoke any more. And no one has given me any money either.' His friend got out a pouch and rolled him a fat fag and bought him a cup of tea from the Chinese greasy spoon nearby.

He reminded me of an old black man called Pius who lived near here in the 'seventies. He was laden with chains and saucepans and bits of metal tied to his clothes. He often sat on the pavement in Talbot Road and if anyone passed he called out, 'Gimme twenty pee.' One day Heathcote Williams, who was living nearby at the time and often saw him, when accosted said, 'No Pius. You give me twenty pee'. Pius opened a big bag and took out the money and handed it over. On another occasion he had seen him sitting in a doorway, taking coins from his bag and rolling them across the pavement so they fell into a drain (not twenty pees of course). For a while Pius squatted an empty shop nearby. The landlord threw him out and put a heavy chain and padlock on the door. By the evening the chain was round Pius's neck.

I finished my article on Robert Partridge, the eccentric Corvo forger, and sent it to *The Book Collector*. After a long time the editor rang up and gave me a little lecture about my punctuation — but also said he would like to print it. So I got it out to correct the punctuation and do a bit of fact-checking.

First I showed it to Anthony Rota to see if my recollection of his correspondence with Partridge was correct. Apparently not. He threatened to sue me if I didn't remove his name. Of course I still don't know if his memory is any better than mine. And then David Drummond pointed out that my account of the sale of the 1865 *Alice in Wonderland* was wrong. Wrong date, wrong price, wrong buyer!

It is invariably the case that if one reads in a newspaper something about a person that one knows, there are always mistakes. 'David Butterscotch, bookmaker, 97,' that sort of thing.

It might be safer to stick to fiction.

Love, David

PARIS, 2006

Hôtel Recamier

Dear Howard,

'In denial' is a phrase I keep hearing. Inigo says I am an alcoholic but that it is no good my just giving up drinking. I would still be an alcoholic, but 'in denial'. It is very annoying. But does this apply to other areas of life?

For example, I have never done any painting. Perhaps I'm in denial; all those excuses about not having any paint, the light being wrong, being too lazy, too drunk ... my energy diverted into concealing my gifts.

Recently I have noticed that I am a bit like an alcoholic about letter-writing. I sneak off with my pad and binge off a few pages, blanking out the real world and its problems.

Perhaps the drift of my thinking is that I was never cut out to be a bookseller at all; that I may be 'in denial' over my childhood ambition to be either a Tramp or an Author, or even both like W. H. Davies or John Steinbeck.

Love, David

FOLKESTONE, 31 January 2006

Dear Howard,

I am in the Tavernetta Ristorante. One could say I have been let in.
My voice must have overridden my down-and-out look. Through
the slightly jammed door plastered with credit-card ads, I am back
in the 1950s. Elderly Italian waiters in maroon dinner jackets;
some Italian Victor Sylvester-type music buzzing from old brown
speakers perched on the tasselled brocade pelmets. An elderly
couple arrived just after me at the next table. As they took off their
well-pressed camel and pale green tweeds an old-fashioned smell
of mothballs filled the restaurant.

My hotel across the road has a slot meter in the room for TV
and Teasmaid. No money is required. There *was* an old German
coin about the size of a shilling, the concierge told me, but some
Germans have stolen it. She sent the heart-of-gold barmaid along
with a franc which seems to fit.

Love, David